A Digest Of

Wesleyan
GRACE
THEOLOGY

Preparing · Pardoning · Perfecting

by Donald W. Haynes

Market
Square
BOOKS

A Digest of
Wesleyan Grace Theology
Preparing • Pardoning • Perfecting
by Donald W. Haynes

©2018 Market Square Publishing Company, LLC.
books@marketsquarebooks.com
P.O. Box 23664 Knoxville, Tennessee 37933

ISBN: 978-1-7323092-1-0
Library of Congress: 2018944909

Printed and Bound in the United States of America
Editors: Kevin Slimp & Kristin Lighter
Cover Illustration ©2018 Market Square Publishing, LLC

In Praise of
This Book

Don Haynes is one of those few authors who gets from me an auto-matic read. Whatever he lays down, I pick up. Both a "churchman" and a "scholar," his judgment about the church and discipleship are honest, informed, incisive and judicious. Plus, he expressed his wisdom with guts and gusto. This book is now the first port-of-call for anyone who wants an introduction, a refresher "course," or a group study book on basic Wesleyan theology. Far too few United Methodists can engage comprehensively in conversation about what John Wesley called "the scriptural way of salvation." The more pluralistic and secular US American culture becomes, the more important this little book is.

Leonard "Len" Sweet
Best-selling author, Professor at Drew University, Tabor College,
and Evangelical Seminary, Owner of PreachTheStory.com

Don Haynes is Wesleyan through and through. He knows the rich-ness of the multiple expressions of Wesleyan theology from personal experience. While deeply informed by scholarship, he writes 'plain truth for plain people' in the spirit of the original Wesley as 'folk theolo-gian.' His insightful discussion of grace theology is much needed today.

Lovett H. Weems, Jr.
Distinguished Professor of Church Leadership at
Wesley Theological Seminary, Washington, D.C. and author

A Digest of Wesleyan Theology contains a rich storehouse of insights, challenges, and inspiration emerging from the Wesleyan tradition. The author admirably weaves together original Wesley sources with diverse scholarly interpretations to provide a clear and accessible rendering of core Wesleyan theology.

Bishop Kenneth Carder

Retired United Methodist Bishop, and Adjunct Faculty at Duke Divinity School

Donald Haynes presents the unique contribution of Wesleyan theology in a way that includes history, commentary, and practical application for Christian educators. His personal style of sharing the power of grace and transformation offers inspiration as well as concrete examples advocating the power of the Good News. This is a wonderful tool for all who teach and lead the church into a deeper understanding of the Wesleyan movement.

Bishop Paul L. Leeland

Resident Bishop, Charlotte Area, United Methodist Church, and former bishop of the Montgomery Area

In this engaging, instructive, and inspiring guide, Donald Haynes followed in John Wesley's tracks to encourage any and all struggling with their faith and social conscience to recognize therein God's saving grace at work; to utilize the church's many empowering offices; and to follow the Wesleyan path from Genesis to Revelation, from creation to redemption, from preparing grace through pardoning grace to perfecting grace.

Russell R. Richey

Adjunct Professor of Church History, Duke Divinity School

Don Haynes is a very gifted communicator who has a long ministry as pastor, teacher, and preacher. Inspired by the work and teaching of John Wesley, in this book he gets to the heart of Wesley's theology. In so doing, he explores the wonder of God's love, the abundance of God's grace, and the depths of New Testament Christianity. He speaks of 'experimental divinity' that integrates the head, heart, and life-style. This book is clearly written, easy to read, and spiritual rich. I commend it to Methodists who want to discover their heritage, and to all Christians who are seeking a deeper and stronger faith. We need to discover a living faith, follow the way of salvation, and keep discovering 'grace upon grace' as we grow in the life of discipleship.

Dr. Peter C. Graves

Retired clergy, British Methodist Conference, and former pastor of
Central Methodist Hall in London, Wesley Methodist Church in Cambridge,
and Centenary UMC in Winston Salem, NC

Any reader will profit spiritually from reading Don Haynes' book. The author grapples seriously with the contemporary meaning and application of historic Wesleyan concepts that have always been central to the tradition. The fast moving text is filled with lively personal interpretations and illustrations that will draw the reader into similar grapplings with the Wesleyan view of the biblical gospel, enlivening and enriching their own Christian experience.

Richard P. Heitzenrater

Retired William Kellon Quick Professor of Church History and Wesley Studies,
The Divinity School, Duke University

In this book, Don Haynes helps the reader understand the compli-cated but convincing theology of John Wesley that focuses on Grace, but not at the expense of service and justice. Through confession, forgiveness, sacrament and renewed commitment, Wesleyan theology provides a way forward when there seems no way. Haynes encourages his readers by revealing new hope in the timeless teachings of the father of Methodism.

Dr. Michael Brown

Senior Pastor, Marble Collegiate Church, New York City, and author.

Don Haynes is a gifted author. A Digest of Wesleyan Grace Theology makes John Wesley's thought accessible to the layman without being superficial. The author combines theology with history and commen-tary. This book will be invaluable for the church member or seeker who wants a clear description of John Wesley's theology and for those who teach new members or adult classes. Methodists have a robust theology of grace, and Don Haynes does a masterful job of explaining it.

Dr. Robert Hopkins, M.D.

Chief, Pediatric Pulmonology, Tulane University School of Medicine

Dr. Don Haynes is a clear thinker, a persuasive communicator, and a faithful steward of Wesleyan theology. His writings inform the reader with solid research and thoughtful discussion. You'll enjoy this book and refer to it often.

Dr. Nido Qubein

President, High Point University, author, and professional motivational speaker

This book is written for my children and grandchildren
in hopes that it will help them know and appreciate
their theological heritage:

Aaron Douglas Haynes and his wife, Laura

Carol Haynes Andrews and her husband, John

Alyssa Joan Haynes Eddy

Alexander Chesson Haynes and his wife, Lauren

Rev. Benjamin Parker Haynes, his wife, Alisha,
and their son, Wesley Chesson

John Bradley Andrews

Christopher Haynes Andrews and his wife, Brooke

Samuel Madison Haynes, II

Jacob Haynes Eddy

Rachel Elizabeth Eddy

AND

My wife of sixty-two years

Joan Parker Haynes
Who by precept and example exonerates perfecting grace.

IN MEMORIAM

My Mother,

Treva Williams Haynes
**(Who said to me when I left for college, "As far back as we
know, our people have been Methodists.")**

Table of Contents

Wesleyan Grace Theology

Preface

Methodism began in England as a via media or "middle way" between John Wesley's Anglo-Catholic life of rigorous self discipline and what he called "experimental and practical divinity." In America, it was a middle way between The Church of England, a liturgical state church, and the Second Great Awakening, an evangelical revival movement. The first generation of Methodists did not use the word "orthodoxy" because John Wesley did not like the term! Dr. Robert Cushman of Duke University correctly documented that the more accurate theological description of the first generations of Methodism is "consensus fidelium"—a consensus of faith.

Wesley was Arminian, not Calvinist. This meant we believe that Jesus died for all humanity, not just the Elect. Wesley also gave Methodism an ecumenical stamp with his practice of ministry and his sermon, *Catholic Spirit,* this book's last chapter. His text was from the Israelite "hell driver" Jehu's words to Jehonadab–"If thy heart is as mine, give me thy hand." (II Kings 10:15 [NIV]) Wesley then added the theological mantra of Methodism: "If we cannot think alike, can we not love alike?"

John Wesley, like John Calvin, believed that God is omnipotent and sovereign. However, Wesley believed that what he called "God's darling attribute" was Love. Love trumps power. He embraced Scripture as primary, dug deeply in the wells of tradition, employed reason, and recognized experience with the resultant paradigm called "grace theology." Grace is grace, but God expresses grace differently in the different seasons of our

1

spiritual lives. Wesley called it "grace upon grace." We call it "preparing grace, pardoning grace, and perfecting grace."

Until the 1850's, American Methodism's growth in influence and membership was phenomenal. According to Dr. Nathan Hatch, president of Wake Forest University, Methodism grew from little more than a footnote in late colonial America to constitute 34% of all Christian church membership by 1840.[1] During those incredible decades, most Methodist preachers, with no formal education, used their "consensus of faith" to motivate a missional evangelism that permeated the American frontier. Socio-economically, according to Dr. Hatch and others, Methodists helped to give political shape and social substance to Jacksonian democracy and free enterprise economics. According to Hatch, Methodism created and defined the emerging "Middle Class" of American society.

While John Wesley was an Oxford graduate and a faculty member of Oxford's Lincoln College, he became a folk theologian. His "experimental divinity" reached and reflected the minds and life circumstances of university philosophers, Anglican bishops, coal miners, factory workers, a diversity of women and men with whom he corresponded, and conversations with "boys at the pub." That practicality and diversity in later generations made Methodism overly susceptible to following cultural trends:

The South was seduced by cultural blindness toward slavery and later to segregation.

Lacking seminaries here or in England, our first theologically educated clergy went to Germany where no one ever heard of John Wesley! Wesleyan theology was almost pre-empted by the philosophy of religion. Wesley was not "recovered" until the 1960's.

By the 1890's our Sunday School curriculum followed public school education into the "progressive education philosophy" of John Dewey!

---

1 Hatch, Nathan, *Methodism and the Shaping of American Culture*, Kingswood, 2001, 27.

Historian Russell Richey has said that while Methodist emphasis in the nineteenth century was missions and evangelism, in the twentieth century it became ecumenism.

We were so enamored with mergers that William Abraham wrote that when The United Methodist Church was formed in 1968, the Methodists were suffering from "doctrinal amnesia." Obsession with mergers also means that we did not help detect the social volcanoes of the 1960's, and did not help prepare for them. Frank Baker in England and Albert Outler of Southern Methodist University became the pioneer scholars for the recovery of Wesley; many others followed. They launched the monumental *Bicentennial Edition of the Works of John Wesley*. Randy Maddox has noted that since the early volumes of that collection, "Wesley scholarship has blossomed dramatically since 1960." [2]

As this is written, the United Methodist Council of Bishops has been presented with three options for a "way forward" for the approximately 7,000,000 members for whom they will speak. Neither option can likely prevent considerable losses in membership as we in a sense redefine our polity and the social justice dimension of our theology. We hope prayerfully that Lyle Schaller was wrong in the title of one of his latest books: *The Ice Cube is Melting*. The intent of the following pages is to provide content for a conversation about a "way forward" with more light and less heat.

Donald W. Haynes

Asheboro, North Carolina

2018

---

[2] Maddox, Randy, *Responsible Grace*, Kingswood, 1994, 24.

Wesleyan Grace Theology

Introduction

"By rule they eat, by rule they drink,

Do all things else by rule, they think –

Method alone must guide 'em all,

Whence Methodists themselves they call." [3]

The message of Methodism has been blurred. William Abraham, a son of Irish Methodism who now teaches at Perkins School of Theology, laments Methodism's "doctrinal amnesia." [4] Russell Richey, a preeminent historian of American Methodism, said in a 2009 Wesley Study Seminar, "The emphasis of Methodism in the nineteenth century was missions and evangelism, and in the twentieth century was ecumenism." I believe the hour has come, in the words of Isaac, to "redig the wells of our fathers" and restate Methodism's fundamentals. We can be appreciative of other communions without losing the identity of our own.

Unlike Calvin who systematically wrote his "dogmatics," John Wesley was a preacher whose theology developed as his personal faith journey matured. During Wesley's years of "Oxford Methodism," he followed Jesus through personal and social holiness as an austere and disciplined life. This chapter of his theological evolution came to a cathartic climax with his exposure to the Moravians and his parish trauma in Geor-

---

3 Luccock, Halford, et.al., *The Story of Methodism*, Abingdon, 1928, 58.

4 Abraham, William, *Waking from Doctrinal Amnesia*, Abingdon, 1995, 12.

gia (1725-1737). Then came May 24, 1738, when he felt his heart "strangely warmed," three days after his brother Charles experienced, "love divine, all loves excelling, joy of heaven to earth come down."

The longest season of John Wesley's preaching was from early 1739 until his death in 1791. As is true of any preacher, the context of his sermons changed both from within himself, in the Methodist movement, Anglicanism, Puritanism, Enlightenment philosophy, and the formation of The United States of America. He finally gave American independence his blessing, calling it "a very uncommon train of providence." Most magnanimously for an old Tory, he then wrote that the American Methodists were, "totally disentangled both from the State and from the English hierarchy." He gave them what was tantamount to his blessing: "They are now at full liberty simply to follow the Scriptures and the Primitive Church. They should stand fast in that liberty, wherewith God has so strangely made them free." [5]

In his posthumously published book, *Experimental Divinity,* Robert Cushman of Duke Divinity School documented that early Methodism was clear about its doctrine, but not in the form of a creed. He called this consensus of faith *consensus fidelium.*[6] He wisely proclaims that this consensus "embodies the 'sufficient reason' for a church's being" and prophesies that "the dimming, or decline, or erosion of that consensus is a negative prognosis for the survival of that church, particularly in modern secular society." He questions whether in the absence of this consensus fidelium, any "Christian community can attain or retain a manifest identity and self-understanding, or convey a recognizable or enduring message, or, indeed to survive at all." [7]

We have retained much of our earlier methodology but

---

5 Telford, John, ed., *The Letters of the Rev. John Wesley,* Epworth Press, 1931, Vol. 7, 238-239.

6 Op. Cit, Cushman, Robert, *John Wesley's Experimental Divinity,* Kingswood, 1969, 100.

7 Ibid., 186.

have let our message erode. While early Methodism allowed a modicum of liberty of conscience in one's interpretation of Scripture, Wesley's "catholic spirit" did not allow theological relativism. Indeed, Wesley warned against being "driven to and fro and tossed about with every wind of doctrine." He was clear:

> "You who call yourselves of 'catholic spirit' only because you are of a muddy understanding, because your mind is all in a mist, because you have no settled, consistent principles; be convinced that you have missed the way; you know not where you are. You think you are into the Spirit of Christ when in truth, you are nearer the spirit of antichrist. Go first and learn the basic elements of the gospel of Christ; and then shall you learn to be of a truly catholic spirit." [8]

In his sermon, *The Way to the Kingdom,* he thundered,

> "Neither does religion consist in orthodoxy or right opinions; which are not in the heart but the understanding. A man may be orthodox at every point; he may not only espouse right opinions, but zealously defend them; he may think justly concerning the Incarnation of our Lord, the ever-blessed Trinity, and every other doctrine contained in holy writ; and yet it is possible he may have no religion at all; and may all the while be as great a stranger as the devil himself to the religion of the heart." [9]

Ted Campbell, Perkins School of Theology professor of church history, is only one of a breed of scholars who took us back to John Wesley. He wrote, "In describing his vision of a 'catholic spirit,' John Wesley distinguished between essential doctrines and opinions about theology or church practices." [10]

For Wesley, all doctrine must be what he called "saving

8 Wesley, John, Sermon: *"Catholic Spirit,"* Outler, Albert, ed. *"The Works of John Wesley,* Abingdon, 1985, Vol. 2, 93.

9 Wesley, John, Sermon, *"The Way To the Kingdom,"* Outler, Albert, ed., JWW, Abingdon, 1984, Vol. 1, 220-222.

10 Campbell, Ted, *Methodist Doctrine,* Abingdon, 1999, 19.

doctrine," and all faith must be "living faith," both of which are dimensions of the scriptural way of salvation.

Summarizing the sermon, *The Way To The Kingdom,* Wesley defined "true religion" in this way:

> "God hath spoken to thy heart, 'Be of good cheer, thy sins are forgiven. Thou hast righteousness and peace and joy in the Holy Ghost.' Then the love of God is shed abroad in thy heart. Thou lovest him because he first loved us. And because thou lovest God, thou lovest thy brother also. Indeed thou art changed into that glorious image wherein thou wast created." [11]

Though Wesley's words use the medium of Shakespearean English, their message expresses the essence of Methodism.

The intent of this book is to guide the individual reader or the small group in a recovery of John Wesley's "experimental divinity." We use the term "Methodist" generically rather than to identify a specific denomination. Wesley's grace theology formed, and still influences, the doctrine of all denominations whose doctrinal heritage is Arminian rather than Calvinist. In his old age, as Wesley was laying the cornerstone of Wesley Chapel in London, he repeated a question asked of him a half century earlier when Methodism was a fledgling movement within Anglicanism:

Q. *What is Methodism? Is it not a new religion?*

A. Nothing could be further from the truth. Methodism; is the old religion, the religion of the Bible, the religion of the primitive Church; none other than the love of God and of all mankind.[12] (By "primitive church," Wesley was referring to the church in the Book of Acts.)

---

11 Op. Cit., Wesley, Sermon, *"The Way to the Kingdom,"* Outler, JWW, Vol. 1, 231.

12 Wesley, John, Sermon, *""On Laying of Foundation of The New Chapel,"* JWW, Outler, Vol. 3, , 585.

Former Duke Divinity School Dean Robert Cushman quotes from and then comments on Wesley's letter to an agnostic lay person at Cambridge named Conyers Middleton:

"To believe (in the Christian sense) is, then, to have a clear sight of God, and confidence in the most High, reconciled to me through the Son of his Love."'

Cushman reflected:

"Accordingly, it is manifest to the Wesleys that the believer has a sure confidence that his sins are forgiven and he is reconciled. Wesley had not known this himself until 1738, but he then found it to be the fundamental doctrine of the Church, the 'scriptural way of salvation,' and, along with sanctification, the 'core doctrine of experimental and practical divinity.'" [13]

Faith for Wesley was grounded in God's indefatigable, universal love. We are not saved by faith but by our faith in God's grace. Grace is what the Book of James cites as "coming down from the Father of lights." We acknowledge that God's light shines from many lamps. As God revealed to Peter, "God shows no partiality." As Dr. Gail O'Day interprets John 14:6, "It is God, the only Son, who is close to the Father's heart, who has made him known." [14] Jesus does not say, 'No one comes to God except through me,' but 'no one comes to the Father except through me.' Christians had to carve out a new religious home for themselves, a home grounded in the incarnation." [15]

Wesley scholar and theologian, Albert Outler, must be given massive credit for calling Methodism to recover John Wesley's theology. Outler wrote, "Wesley offers a treasure to the church

---

13 Op. Cit., Cushman, 21.

14 O'Day, Gail, *The New Interpreter's Bible*, Abingdon, 1955, Vol. IX, 744.

15 Ibid. 744.

of tomorrow that will leave it poorer if ignored." [16]

In the 21st century to date, most neo-evangelicals reflect Calvinism, not Arminianism, as they "write the script" for seekers of saving grace. Fundamentalists also influence bright young students on university campuses. "Grace upon grace" theology is less a guilt trip and more a liberating experience. The intent of these pages is to nudge Wesley into the discussion of what it means to see salvation as "preparing, pardoning, and perfecting grace." Jesus met each person where she or he was. He did not have a cookie-cutter message or approach, nor should we. We do not encourage a prescription-like "sinner's prayer," or "four spiritual laws," because we see neither of these in Jesus' own evangelism. Jesus began in relationship and remained there. We must be like him in retaining a core value; that core value is the uniqueness and sanctity of every child of God.

As Randy Maddox, Professor of Theology and Methodist Studies at Duke Divinity School, reminds us, "Wesley insisted on a dynamic interrelationship between God's justifying grace and our cooperant response." [17] Wesley connected cooperant dimensions of the "scriptural way of salvation." Maddox calls this "synergism" or the synergy of God's "saving grace" with our "living faith." As we shall see, this response is an expression of human free will.

Wesley summarized his theology as "grace upon grace." After prevenient grace he used the metaphor of "porch" for repentance, "threshold" for the experience of saving grace, and perfecting grace as God's leading us to "every room of the house" of our thoughts, words, and deeds. By this metaphor of "house," Wesley meant that God seeks to perfect us in love in every dimension of our life. We cannot grow in grace without spiritual discipline in a faith community. Stated another way as we shall see in the following pages, God seeks and finds us, and

---

16 Outler, Albert, *Evangelism and Theology in the Wesleyan Spirit*, Discipleship Resources, 2000, 111.

17 Op. Cit., Maddox, 150.

calls us to repent of our sins, and saves us with a sense of God's redeeming love. The work of the Holy Spirit cannot be rigidly doctrinalized. Grace theology calls us and empowers us to love God and neighbor without reservation or retribution. Wesley's was an ecumenical love. He said more than once, "Though we might not think alike, can we not love alike?" We must practice a radical hospitality that includes personal follow-up of worship guests and interpersonal faith sharing.

The bottom line is that not until the "grace upon grace" that follows our acceptance of Jesus as our Savior and Lord will we have what Charles Wesley called "Love divine, all loves excelling, joy of heaven to earth come down." In 1926, Gilbert Rowe of Duke Divinity School wrote in his volume, *The Meaning of Methodism,* "The culminating doctrine of Methodism is the witness of the Spirit." [18]

Essential in the Methodist message is the inseparability of doctrines and personal discipline. Being saved must be followed by growth in grace, which expresses itself in the ethics of Micah 6:8, Jesus' "Sermon on the Mount," his parable in Matthew 25, and the discipline of Ephesians 6. Through Bishop Reuben Job and others, we are recovering this imperative to "walk the walk."

Some use the term "God's plan of salvation." I demur. "Plan" is a corporate term. Others refer to Wesley's *ordo salutis.* Again, I demur because Wesley himself used the term, *via salutis* or "way of salvation." "Way" is a relational term. Saying "Jesus has forgiven me of my sins" is just the first step in the way of salvation, not *fait accompli.* God relates to us in the various seasons and circumstances of our lives and through what St. Paul called "the spirit of adoption" in which we call God, "Father." *(In reality, Paul's term for us to use is "Abba." Abba was the term of endearment used by Palestinian children in Jesus' day as they addressed their paternal parent.)*

Dr. Cushman closed the last book he ever wrote with ominous words:

---

18 Rowe, Gilbert, *The Meaning of Methodism,* Cokesbury, 1926, 151.

"By the close of the 19th century, Wesley's 'experimental divinity'—the Scriptural way of salvation—had lost currency. By the third quarter of the 20th century, a 'consensus faith' was not regarded by many Methodists as essential and its affirmation was seen as controversial. Meanwhile the spectacular decline of membership in The United Methodist Church may suggest that many have wearied beyond endurance with a church that manages mainly the 'form of godliness' on the one hand, and that seems doctrinally shapeless on the other." [19]

We must hear that message.

In *The Faith We Declare*, Edwin Lewis wrote in 1939, "'In Christ' is the relationship by whose light we read God, and in whose light we will read ourselves." [20] Nearly eighty years later, this remains a Methodist fundamental. The world is waiting for a church that can declare its faith!

Theology that is "grace upon grace" is not static; it does not "cabin, crib, and confine" the work of the Holy Spirit. Wesley broke with the Moravians on July 20, 1740 because he insisted that people can have "degrees of faith." Importantly though, if we present this as evidence that Methodists can believe just anything, we err. This does not mean that we are a theological sieve or that we must remain mute about our beliefs. Wesley scholar and theologian Albert Outler established this for us with his insistence that Methodism has "a marrow of doctrine" that can be identified and that must be conserved. [21] This language is in the "Theological Statement" in *The Book of Discipline*.

The bottom line: Methodism has a doctrine, but we believe that true religion is not limited either to rational conclusions

---

19 Op. Cit., Cushman, 1989, 188-189.

20 Lewis, Edwin, *The Faith We Declare*, Cokesbury, 1939, 117.

21 *The Book of Discipline, The United Methodist Church*, The United Methodist Publishing House, 2016, "Our Doctrinal Heritage. 50.

of the head or the enthusiasm of the heart. We believe in a marriage of the cognitive and the emotive, the head and the heart. Depending upon the stage of his own journey, Wesley can be quoted to document either position. Randy Maddox clarifies this: "The mature Wesley integrated sacramentalist and evangelical emphases." This book will take the reader down this road of "grace upon grace." To "stay on the road," Wesley outlined what he called "means of grace." An entire chapter will detail those "means."

Author Diane Butler Bass, a former United Methodist herself, wrote in *Christianity for the Rest of Us,* "Few United Methodists can provide a conversational synopsis of 'who' the UMC is!" We want in the following pages to provide such a conversational synopsis! Between churches centered in sacramentalism and churches centered in enthusiasm, Methodism is a middle way.

God's light shines from many lamps. We therefore hope that this book will be helpful to those whose spiritual journey is not Methodist, or even Christian. It is for all who look to God's Word as the "lamp for our feet and a light for our pathway." If you are searching the Scriptures for your own salvation, or on the journey in search of a meaningful life, may God use John Wesley to lead you to what Wesley called "trust and confidence" in God's love when your faith might falter.

Questions for Discussion and Reflection

What was said about Methodism that prompted you to respond, "Amen! This is what I have been looking for!"

What prompted you to think, "Hmm. I never thought that way before. Interesting and helpful."

What bothered you most in this introduction?

What quote did you highlight as new to your previous knowledge of Wesley or his disciples?

How does your journey reflect the path of what Wesley called "grace upon grace?" Do you have a vivid memory of being saved? Has most of your spiritual growth come through "God's nudge through your conscience," or someone's witness to you, or your study of the Bible?

Was all this "spiritual journey" talk rather foreign to yours? Were the references to "holiness" or "perfecting grace" new terms to you? If you heard about them or experienced these doctrines in other denominations, did you know of their origins in Methodism?

Do you consider yourself a celebrant of God's amazing, saving grace?

Does this introduction give you some clarity as to what the "consensus of faith" (consensus fidelium) is for Methodism?

What in the Introduction motivated you to turn anew to Scriptures with which you had never done any homework?

Do you plan to continue reading the rest of the book?

Are you in a group who will read the book together?

Chapter One

Genesis 1:27
Tells You Who We Really Are

"Then God said, 'Let us make man in our image, according to our likeness; and let them rule over the fish of the sea, and the birds of the air, over the livestock, over all the{wild animals}, and over all the creatures that move along the ground. So God created man in his own image, in the image of God he created him; male and female he created them. And God blessed them.... God saw all that he had made, and it was very good."

Genesis 1:26-27, 31 (NIV) [22]

In the theology and in the preaching of Western Christianity, this is the most overlooked verse of scripture in the Bible that would substantially change our view of human nature and our understanding of salvation. John Wesley preached on this text on November 15, 1730 in St. Mary's Church on the Oxford University campus. Quite a number of faculty members were in the congregation. Obviously, Wesley had done some digging in the college libraries of Oxford University and found the work of Eastern Orthodox theologians as well as the work of Roman Catholic theologians. The Greeks, taking Genesis 1:27 literally, assumed that humans were originally innocent, but not complete until and unless their communion with their Creator

---

22 ('adam" means "man." As footnotes correctly indicate in the *New Revised Standard Version*, the Hebrew word " humankind" in that translation is not literal Hebrew. "The pronoun translated "them" is in Hebrew the male gender, "him." Also, the word translated "cattle" is more correct in the NIV. It is a generic word meaning "livestock.").

matured. Two gifts came with our being made in God's image: self-consciousness and self-determination.

The most profound question you will ask yourself in your whole life will be, 'Who am I?' Robert Burns, the Scot, wrote, "Oh wad some power the Giftie gie us to see ourselves as others see us." Indeed, God did give us that introspective power! When I was a college freshman, a speaker at chapel captured my attention by using a picturesque "attention getter" to introduce his lecture on psychology. To explain the contrast between humankind and the rest of the animal kingdom, he said, "Let me explain it this way. A jackass cannot step outside itself and looking back on itself say, 'I am a jackass.' On the other hand, a man has the God-given capacity to step outside himself, look back on himself and say, 'I am a jackass.'" After the chuckles died down among the students, Dr. Evans continued. "That," he said, "is self-consciousness."

The other dimension of the *Imago Dei* is self-determination. We have a will with which to determine free choices. Choices invariably set in motion a process of consequences. In the Garden of Eden story, the 'game-changer' event was Adam and Eve's decision to eat the fruit of the "tree that would make them like God." The power to do that is self-determination. That decision determined the loss of their original righteousness and became what we theologically call "original sin."

When I was a college senior, the speaker was Dr. E. Stanley Jones, a Methodist missionary who had spent his entire long life in India, ministering in a culture where the predominant religion was Hinduism. Dr. Jones also left me with a life-long memory with this quote: "When God goes, life goals go, and when life goals go, life meaning goes." I cannot totally agree with Dr. Jones. When God goes life goals do not go; they change. Many goals are dead end alleys. Psalm 19 portrays Jewish wisdom on this subject, identifying the life goals that bring good consequence:

> *"The law of the Lord is perfect,*
> *reviving the soul..*

The decrees of the Lord are trustworthy,
making wise the simple.
The precepts of the Lord are right,
giving joy to the heart.
The commands of the Lord are radiant,
giving light to the eyes.
The fear of the Lord is pure,
enduring forever..
The decrees of the Lord are firm,
and all of them are righteous.
They are more precious than gold,
than much pure gold;
they are sweeter than honey,
than honey from the honeycomb...
May these words of my mouth and this meditation of my
heart be pleasing in your sight,
Lord, my rock and my redeemer"

Psalm 19:7-10, 14 (NIV)

Very, very few Western theologians pay even scant note to the meaning of Genesis 1:27. In his sermon, "The Image of God," Wesley interpreted God's crowning creation as men and women created with perfectly accurate understanding and insight into the rest of creation. In Randy Maddox words, Wesley believed that "Humans were originally created capable of participating in God, and when they do, they embody God's moral character and find fulfillment." A Methodist fundamental therefore is our belief in "original righteousness" on the morning of creation. Wesley's exegesis of Genesis 1:27 was that humankind have three dimensions of the image of God—the natural image, the political image, and the moral image. Wesley saw this having three dimensions:

The natural dimension is our brain, which is capable of reason, intuitive creativity, and other cognitive faculties. One aspect of this "natural image" is basic survival instinct.

The political dimension of being like God is the liberty of making decisions through our choices of behavior and emotions (which he called "affections.") One aspect of this image of God is what Wesley called "relational anthropology." That is, by our exercise of free will, we establish relationships with other persons, with the rest of creation, and with God. According to the excellent explanation of Wesley at this point, this is our liberty to keep or squander Adam's first estate. In that sense, Mr. Wesley preached, "Man is the sole lord and sovereign judger of his own actions." Our exercise of the political image of God results in good choices that for the most part have good consequences and bad choices that for the most part have bad consequences. This means that the essence of "love of God and love of other persons" is living out this "political image" of our Creator. Unless God had "graced us with liberty," as Wesley put it, we would have only the survival instincts of animals. "From Wesley's perspective, it was absurd to think that God's sovereignty was in any way diminished by allowing people a measure of freedom and responsibility." [23]

Dr. Nido Qubein, president of High Point University, drums into the minds of the students, "Good choices bring good consequences; bad choices bring bad consequences." Well said! Herein lay both the potential and the danger of self-determination. Theologically, it is usually called "free will" and Wesley calls it one dimension of being created in the image of God.

The moral dimension of being created in the image of God is our conscience. Randy Maddox of Duke Divinity School discovered Wesley's beautiful term for conscience– "our inmost soul." In recent times, someone has defined conscience as the innate "traffic light" of our moral and ethical options—to go, to proceed with great caution, or to stop! This is what Paul inferred in Romans 1:20-23. There, Paul wrote:

"For since the creation of the world, God's invisible qualities—his eternal power and divine nature—have been clearly seen, being understood from what has been made, so that people are without excuse. For although they knew God, they neither glorified him as God nor gave thanks

---

23 Thorsen, Don, *Calvin vs. Wesley,* Abingdon, 2013, 10.

to him, but their thinking became futile and their foolish hearts were darkened. Although they claimed to be wise, they became fools and exchanged the glory of the immortal God for images made to look like mortal man and birds and animals and reptiles" (NIV).

Paul is saying that our conscience is conditioned by our childhood home, our culture, our religious code of words and actions, and personal relationships. This means that conscience changes, even within each individual's life journey. What we consider a sin in one season or setting of life is permissive in another season, and vice versa.

In 1754, Wesley wrote that he considered women to have been created to be subordinate to men, but in 1765 he wrote that male and female were created by God to be equal in all ways.[24] Any conversation among older adults reveals a vast difference in what we considered right or wrong in 2018 as compared to 1958. Some who find racial segregation abhorrent today must admit tolerating it in 1958. Women were denied by Christian men the right to vote until 1918. Mormons consider the use of caffeine, nicotine, or alcohol a sin that "hurts their conscience," but temperate use of these does not bother the Episcopalians or the Methodists. In Nazi Germany, Lutheran pastor Dietrich Bonhoeffer participated in the assassination plot to murder Adolph Hitler in 1944. So it is that the old adage, "Let your conscience be your guide" does not result in universal behavior patterns.

Wesley did not sugar coat human nature. In the Bible, Adam and Eve broke the sanctity of their communion with God in their power grab to become "as God." Adam's disobedience had a logical consequence; bad choices are followed by bad consequences! This becomes a state of estrangement, a breach of Genesis 1:27. When God called "Adam, where are you?" Adam was hiding and did not answer. Shame and guilt had entered the story. This is what Western and Eastern theology and John Wesley call "the fall." Theologically, this is called "Original

24 Op. Cit. Maddox, 72.

Sin" because by yielding to the tempter, they literally make the "original sin-act."

Quickly in the Bible, we see them deteriorate from relationship to brokenness, from obedience to disobedience, and from responsible stewardship to abusive dominance over the rest of creation. The apostle Paul reiterates the "Eden scene" in Romans 5:12-13a (NIV): *Therefore, just as sin entered the world through one man, and (spiritual) death through sin, and in this way death came to all men, because all sinned—for before the law was given, sin was in the world"*

To summarize Wesley's understanding of our being created in "the image of God," but now "fallen," he identified three states of humanity:

The created state, in the image of God (original righteousness).

The fallen state (universal addiction to sin). The correct translation of Romans 3:23 is, "For all have sinned, and fall short of the glory of God, they are justified freely by his grace through the redemption that came through Jesus Christ" (NIV). (The predicate is not "come short," but "fall short" remembering the Garden of Eden fall).

The restored state (pursuant to our salvation). He defined sin as "dis-ease" and salvation as "taking the cure. He used the terms of the clinic rather than terms of the court. Salvation is a healing process more than a pardon.

Dr. Randy Maddox, uncovering long ignored evidence, pointedly documents that because of our being made originally in God's image, there is a fundamental difference between "Greek" theology and "Latin" theology:

"Western Christianity insists that every human being inherits the guilt of Adam and Eve's original sin and humanity's moral faculties are totally depraved and hopelessly addicted. Eastern Christianity denies this "domino

20

effect." Us theologians insist that the Fall did render us prone to sin, but not incapable of responding to God's offer of healing us from our 'disease.'" [25]

As James Payton documents in his book, *Light From the Christian East,* "Eastern Christianity teaches that the *Imago Dei* is essential to human existence; no one can be a human being without also having the image of God." The dynamics of this setting is a harmonious relationship which Payton calls "unceasing communion with God." That is the very important seminal meaning of Genesis 1:27; it distinguishes humanity from the rest of creation. Nothing else bears that image.

Also importantly, Eastern Christian thought, reflecting Hebrew theology, does not denigrate the human body; it sees the body as integral to human personhood as are the inward and intangible constituents. This is in contrast to Western Christian theology. Also, there is no superiority given men in Genesis 1:27—"male and female" equally bear God's image. [26] The emphasis of Catholic and Reformed (i.e. Calvinist) theology has reflected an "after the Fall" view of human nature. That means that much of our doctrinal influence based our theology of creation on Adam's disobedience rather than God's original creation. This is seen in much preaching and in many of the hymns we sing. However, like Eastern Orthodox theologians, Wesley insisted that we must place much more emphasis on Genesis 1:27 than we have done heretofore. He saw this "creation verse" as a document of humanity's "original righteousness."

John Wesley loved to use the term "being restored" rather than "being saved." I told my seminary classes the difference between two pots in an antique shop that are equally blackened from abuse and neglect. If you place a magnet on pot #1, it sticks, meaning that the pot is cast iron. However, when you place your magnet on pot #2 it does not stick, meaning that the

---

25 Ibid. 74.

26 Payton, James, *Light from the Christian East,* Intervarsity Press, 2007, 107.

pot is brass! You can scrub and clean the cast iron pot all you wish, but it will still be a blackened pot. If, on the other hand, you scrub and clean and polish the brass pot, it will shine beautifully. It is restored to its original pristine beauty. We are like the brass pot—dirty, neglected, and looking like junk, but God does not create junk! God made Adam and Eve in God's own image and still loved them as much as before the Fall, but Adam had estranged himself from that relationship. Adam rejected God's seeking love. This set into perpetual motion what we call "original sin."

Randy Maddox has documented a gradual change in Wesley so that in his "late period," Wesley locates our guilty conscience in our own sins, not in the sin of our ancestors.[27] Wesley did not have the interest in the origin of sin that Calvin had; rather Wesley saw universal evidence of sin as an infection, a 'dis-ease', and being saved as "taking the cure" to make us whole again. Again, the "Cappadocian fathers," Gregory of Nyssa and Gregory of Nazianzus, teach us that sin should be seen as a distortion of God's creation.

Let Jesus illustrate the distinction between universal sin and inherited sin! He did it with his famous apocryphal story that we call "The Parable of the Prodigal Son." Obviously the "waiting father" portrays the love of God for both of his sons. Both sons break his heart, one by prematurely taking his inheritance, leaving home, and ending broke and watching pigs. The other stayed home and worked but his heart was full of grudges, resentment, and eventually jealousy and rage. The boys are representative of all humankind; the expression of our sin is as diverse as our individuality.

To dig a bit more deeply into Jesus' parable, the boy who had wasted his fortune and ruined his life "came to himself." This clearly alludes to the conscience that Wesley called "the inmost soul." Wesley called it an "awakening." He also used the term "whisper" of the Holy Spirit. Leonard Sweet uses the verb "nudge" to describe the work of the Holy Spirit in us, even

---

27 Op. Cit., Maddox, 75.

if we are "soaked in sin." "Nudge" is a good word; some people take a lot of nudges before they "come to themselves" and say, "I am more than I have become; I am going home." On the other hand, some people have one precipitous "God moment" and rise and go to their Father, repenting of their sins. In the parable, Jesus did not indicate the elder son's final response to grace.

The title of one of Randy Maddox' books is *Responsible Grace*. If guilt is inherited from the corporate human race, or if God imputes guilt and damns our souls to hell, then we are not responsible. But if God loves us unconditionally and indeed is the "waiting father" whose love never ends, then our response to God's "nudge" to come home or to remain in the pig sty is our personal responsibility embedded in the freedom of will. Grace is universal, but it is cooperant or synergistic. God loves us. Our response can be to accept God's love or to reject God's love; we have the free will in that monumental decision. Salvation is a relationship between Creator and creature, a relationship between two "beings;" a relationship requiring reciprocity.

Wesley believes that we were created "originally righteous" and in harmony with God and each other. This does not mean that he waffled on the universal malady of human sinfulness.[28] As we shall read in a future chapter, Wesley repeatedly preached and wrote that sin is universal. However, he saw sin as the consequence of the infirmity of human nature. He insisted that God does not will or "impute" sin as an inheritance from Adam's depravity.[29] Sin, to Wesley, was more a consequence of disobeying God rather than a punishment by which we inherit Adam's disobedience. As his mother, Susanna, had written him when he was a college student, "The doctrine of predestination makes God the author of evil."

"Total depravity" as a Calvinistic doctrine means that we are so evil, so enslaved to sin, and so categorically estranged from God that we have no spiritual capacity for "hearing the

---

28 Ibid. 73.

29 Ibid. 79.

still, small voice" or experiencing a "God moment." That is, to the rigid Calvinist, God must "zap us" if we are to be converted; we cannot make a willful, free choice to accept God's love, mercy, and grace.

Wesley rejected total depravity. Both Wesley brothers insisted that just as in Jesus' parable of "The Prodigal Son," every child is loved, every person is a child of God, regardless of current relationship with our heavenly Father. Jesus came to reveal God's love for every human being. Indeed, Jesus' ministry with people, as we find recorded in the Gospels, certainly illustrates that Jesus came not to those who, in his words, "do not need a doctor," but to the ones who do! In other words, Jesus came to seek and to save all humankind.

Charles Wesley has us singing this if we just notice the words: ***Come, Sinners, to the Gospel Feast:***

Come, sinners, to the gospel feast; let every soul be Jesus' guest.

Ye need not one be left behind, for God hath bid all humankind.

Sent by my Lord, on you I call; the invitation is to all.

Come all the world! Come sinner, thou! All things in Christ are ready now.

Come, all ye souls by sin oppressed, ye restless wanderers after rest;

Ye poor, and maimed, and halt, and blind, in Christ a hearty welcome find....

This is the time, no more delay! This is the Lord's accepted day.

Come thou, this moment at his call, and live for him who died for all."

You can see that the language of this Wesleyan hymn, written in 1747 and still in *The United Methodist Hymnal,* is an apt synopsis of Wesley's insistence that every person is among the Elect and that God's will is that "none be left behind." The mission of the gospel is universal salvation. The mission is accomplished as the Holy Spirit awakens a human soul and that person responds positively.

Hymn writer Frederick Faber has us singing, "For the love of God is broader than the measure of the mind; and the heart of the Eternal is most wonderfully kind." John Greenleaf Whittier, the great Quaker, reflects this in a hymn we sing all too seldom: "I know not how the islands lift their fronded palms in air; I only know I cannot drift beyond His love and care." Methodist hymnwriter, Fanny Crosby, also has us sing this theological fundamental in her song, *Rescue the Perishing:* "Down in the human heart, crushed by the tempter, feelings lie buried that grace can restore. Touched by a loving heart, wakened by kindness, chords that were broken can vibrate once more."

In Romans 8:35-39, Paul lists all the things that can go wrong in our lives—hardship, persecution, famine, nakedness, danger, or sword." Then he affirms, "No, in all these things we are more than conquerors through him who loved us." He concludes with the doxology that nothing "will be able to separate us from the love of God that is in Christ Jesus our Lord." God's love is inclusive. We were made in God's indelible image and God's love will not let us go. Whatever we do to waste this precious life that is given us, "we cannot drift beyond God's love and care."

Let us never forget the seminal importance of Genesis 1:27. "Made in the image of God" is stamped indelibly upon our eternal soul. Sin is incredibly disruptive, but cannot sever the tie between the Creator and the created. No matter how much heartache or embarrassment a wayward child brings to parents, the love bond cannot be broken. He or she is still their child. So it is with God; we are still God's children, whatever our behavioral pattern, or however many dreams we have shattered.

Questions for Discussion and Reflection

When you ask yourself, "Who am I?" do you think of your answer as being "I am a child of God, made in the image of God?"

Do you think of the effects of your sin as guilt or what Wesley called "dis-ease" or "infirmity of the soul" and what Randy Maddox calls a "malady?"

Do you believe that it is God's will that, in Charles Wesley's words in his hymn, "not one be left behind?"

If not, do you believe that God's will is that some be condemned to hell? If you believe that God elects some for heaven and some for hell, have you lost a loved one whom you think is lost for all eternity?

Which metaphor do you prefer—the judgment of "GUILTY" and sentencing of the court or "DIS-EASE" and the healing and restoration of the clinic?

Is sin something we inherit from Adam, or are we possessed by the devil? Or is sin our bad choices in response to the enticements of temptation?

What is your personal interpretation of Genesis 1:27?

"He (God) made man in his own image, a spirit endued with understanding and liberty. Man, abusing that liberty, produced evil and brought sin and pain into the world. God permitted this in order to give us a fuller manifestation of his wisdom, justice, and mercy by bestowing on all who would receive it an infinitely greater happiness."

John Wesley, 1782

"...Man is very far gone from original righteousness and is of his own nature inclined to evil....And this infection doth remain...whereby the lust of the flesh is not subject to the Law of God."

Article of Religion IX–"Of Original or Birth Sin"

"In 1759, John Wesley reformulated an earlier treatise and preached a new sermon entitled, "Original Sin." In 1766 he insisted that this and two other sermons be required reading for all Methodist preachers. In his mind, therefore, and in the logic of his soteriology (doctrine of salvation), this sermon is a major doctrinal statement in which he sought to compound the Latin tradition of total depravity with the Eastern Orthodox view of sin as disease and of salvation as "taking the cure." This sermon documents that Wesley was not a Pelagian."

**Albert Outler, *The Works of John Wesley*,
Abingdon, 1985, V. 2, 171**

Chapter Two

Sin is Real.
The Evidence is Clear!

"All have sinned and fall short of the glory of God."
Romans 3:23

*"I see another law at work in my members of my body,
waging war against the law of my mind and making me a
prisoner of the law of sin at work within my members.
What a wretched man I am! Who will rescue me from this
body of death?"*
St. Paul as he "came to himself,"
Romans 7:23-24 (NIV)

On our journey of salvation, our sense of sinfulness comes
as a major dimension of a "God moment" when we come face to
face with the folly of "doing it our way" with our personal lives.
Like the "Prodigal Son" in Jesus' parable, we "come to ourself."
When we look into the mirror of our own soul, we see a self
centeredness that might be expressed as arrogance, as narcis-
sism, or as low self esteem. In Isaiah 6:5, the young prophet was
in the temple and "saw the Lord." When he sensed God's holy
presence, Isaiah said, "Woe is me! I am lost for I am a man of
unclean lips and I live among a people of unclean lips; yet my
eyes have seen the King, the Lord of Hosts."

The universal sin of which Romans 3:23 speaks refers obviously to the universality of our state as sinners. In the words of
Wesley's commentary, we have "fallen short of God's image for

29

us." The word "fall" refers to the common state of humankind. Wesley uses the term "original righteousness" to reflect our being made in the image of God (Genesis 1:27 {NIV}) and therefore sees salvation as restoration or healing following the fall.

Jesus said, "Anyone who has seen me, has seen the Father." (John 14:9 {NIV}). As God stepped onto the stage of human history in the birth of Jesus, we saw God's true character: "God so loved the world that he gave his one and only Son that whoever believes in him shall not perish but have eternal life." (John 3:16 {NIV}) Now we must ask, "Just what kind of mess did God come into?" This brings us to the doctrine of Original Sin or "birth sin." Though we disagree with those who say that our sinful state is "No. 1," we also disagree with those who do not see the seriousness of sin.

First, let's be clear about the "signs of the times" in which Wesley developed his theology of grace. The universities were dominated by the philosophy known as "The Enlightenment." A host of brilliant men updated much of Greek philosophy. In Dr. Albert Outler's words, "It was a cherished conviction that men, once freed from their superstitious errors, would recover their innate moral virtue, viz. the power to will the good and to do it." [30] Wesley says, "Accounts of this kind have particularly abounded in the present century. Here not a few persons of strong understanding and extensive learning have employed their utmost abilities to show what they termed 'the fair side of human nature.' If their accounts of him be just, man is 'a little less than God.'" [31] ... So it is now quite unfashionable to talk otherwise, to say anything disparaging about human nature. [32]

Wesley then asks, "In the meantime, what must we do with our Bibles? For they will never agree with this." [33] This informed opinion documents that Wesley saw the error in the

---

30 Outler, Albert, *The Works of John Wesley*, Abingdon, 1985, Vol. 2, 170.

31 Ibid., Wesley, John, Sermon, "Original Sin," JWW, Vol. 2, 172.

32 Ibid., 173.

33 Ibid., 173.

philosophy of the Enlightenment – a philosophy that would later erode the doctrine of original sin in Methodist Sunday school literature and Methodist seminaries. From the late 19th century the wide and deep influence of the social sciences of psychology, sociology, and economics made the doctrine of sin either archaic or harmful. We saw this influence in the public school curricula which reflected John Dewey's progressivism. While we owe considerable debt to the social sciences, we must again ask the question that Wesley posed, "But what shall we do with our Bibles?" Sin is real.

Edwin Lewis of Drew University called Methodism back from the "Enlightenment safari" with his book, *A Christian Manifesto,* in 1934: "Christianity is a religion of regeneration. You will believe again in the necessity and possibility of human nature being changed. The necessity of the change is in the fact of sin, both as a status and a deed; the possibility of change is in the nature of the grace of God... Deny the doctrine of sin and you will deny much more than that. Christian truth has a certain organic character. Change anywhere affects change everywhere. Is it that the old terms are dropped because people have ceased to believe in what those terms represent?" [34] Lewis tried valiantly to bring original sin back to the sermon!

Edwin Lewis was not alone. Shelton Smith, Professor of "History of Protestant Thought" at Duke, wrote six months before Pearl Harbor in 1941 regarding John Dewey's insistence on the *infinite value of human personality*:

"From the standpoint of the Christian faith, there seems to be no ground on which to say that human personality is of 'infinite worth.' Man is a contingent creature; in the Christian faith man is a theonomous being, deriving his meaning and value from his relation to God. When human personality is elevated to 'infinite value,' humanity is deified–made as gods."[35]

---

34 Lewis, Edwin, *A Christian Manifesto,* Abingdon, 1934, 111.

35 Smith, H. Shelton, *Faith and Nurture,* Scribners, 1941, 44, 46.

He warned, "Those religious educators who renounce a theocentric interpretation of the human situation are quite right in discarding the term 'sin.' They look only to the empirical sciences for their terms. Therefore they decline to speak of sin in its tragic dimensions. For sin becomes really tragic only to those who interpret it from the divine perspective." [36]

Lewis spoke prophetically a word that is an integral part of this book: "The time has come when the church must assert again...its right to deliver its soul on the great issues of life without first obtaining permission from some other sources." [37] Methodist Sunday School editors ignored the warnings of Lewis and Smith to our peril. Not until the 1960's were we hearing the trumpet sound again the doctrine of original sin. It was Albert Outler from SMU who shouted, "Something has gone fearfully awry in the human enterprise." [38] The doctrine of sin is fundamental; it affects every dimension of our theology.

Wesley insists that the doctrine of original sin is what separates Christianity from all other religions. His text for the Original Sin sermon is Genesis 6:5, which ends, "and that every inclination of the thoughts of his heart was only evil all the time." Wesley's comment on that verse is, "Allow this and you are so far a Christian; deny it, and you are but a heathen still." [39]

If we are not sinners, we need no salvation! But we are sinners; our predicament is that of Paul in Romans 7 – "Is there no one who can do anything for me? That is the real question." (Romans 7:24 {The Message}).

In his sermon "Original Sin," Wesley supported St. Paul's conclusion: "So long as men remain in their natural blindness of understanding, they are not sensible of their spiritual wants." Wesley says we can "acknowledge [God's] being, but

---

36 Ibid. 99.

37 Op. Cit., Lewis *The Faith We Declare*, 134.

38 Op. Cit., Outler, 29.

39 Op. Cit. Wesley, Sermon, "Original Sin," JWW, Vol, 2, 184.

have no acquaintance of Him. We can know there is an emperor of China, yet we do not know him." [40] Wesley means we can have a cognitive belief in God but no personal relationship.

Steve Harper can be our teacher here by eliciting certain salient fundamentals from the whole of Wesley's writings:

"If sin were a 'thing' we could escape it, but because it is an infection, the only option is healing. We cannot try enough, learn enough, worship enough, or do enough good works to heal ourselves. Outside help is the only possible solution. The problem of sin infects the very nature of what it means to be human. Any attempts to remove ourselves from it are only exercises in futility. The solution is transformation, not escape. Wesley can help us out of our futile efforts to treat sin as a 'thing.' He keeps using the term 'disease' and pointing out that the only solution is 'taking the cure.'" [41]

According to Wesley, what are the symptoms of sin? Sin makes us dead toward God. It gives us a false sense of security and peace. Wesley said:

"The poor, unawakened sinner has no knowledge of himself. He knows not that he is a fallen spirit. Full of disease that he is, he fancies himself in perfect health. Bound in misery and iron, he dreams he is happy and at liberty contented in his fallen state, to live and die without knowing he is made in the image of God, ignorant both of his disease and the only remedy for it." [42]

Wesley in another sermon asks, "Are you able to change your own heart from sin to holiness? No more than you are able to quicken a dead body!" [43] Then he gives us the good

40 Ibid.177.

41 Harper, Steve, *John Wesley's Message for Today*, Zondervan, 1983, 32.

42 Wesley, Sermon, *"Awake, Thou that Sleepest,"* Outler, JWW, V. 1, 143.

43 Op. Cit., 226, Sermon, *"The Way to the Kingdom,"* JWW, Vol 1, 229.

news—that if we have "sorrow of heart" and lift up our eyes to heaven, "Thou art not far from the kingdom of God."

Sin is self-captivity. Thinking ourselves free, we become captives of our own reason, desires, prejudice, cultural blindness, and raw lusts – "prey to our own weaknesses." We are like Frank Sinatra sang in 1964 of his story: "I did it my way." He bragged that he was the master of his fate and kneeled to no one! In this state, we recognize no need for a Redeemer; there is nothing to be forgiven of. When we reach this low spiritual ebb, sin enjoys a reign of terror and wreaks havoc in our lives and those whom we influence most.

Sin is helplessness in the effort to change. Wesley did not believe that the image of God in which we are created is destroyed, but he thought it rendered powerless. Sin has done that to us. Wesley said, "Though he strive with all his might, he cannot conquer; sin is mightier than he." [44] Let us call for a reality check; we cannot pull ourselves up by our own bootstraps – the metaphor itself is ridiculous if one is sinking in quicksand. Our "free will" at this point is impotent. God's grace is essential.

Sin is our judgment of others. Did not Jesus say, "With the judgment you make you will be judged, and the measure you give will be the measure you get." In *The Shack,* Mack is told that his judgment is to become the Judge! He is told:

> "You have judged many throughout your life. You have judged actions and motivations of others as if you really knew! You have judged the color of skin, body language, and body odor. You have judged history and relationships. You have judged beauty and righteousness by your concepts. By all accounts, you are quite well practiced in the activity." [45]

The Achilles' heel of 19th-century liberalism was looking at human nature through rose-colored glasses. Overlooking the "bent to sinning," liberal theology blamed the environment

---

44 Wesley, John, Sermon, *"The Spirit of Bondage and Adoption,"* JWW, Vol 1, 258.

45 Young, William Paul, *The Shack,* Windblown Press, 2007, 185.

for everything wrong in society, from personal sin to systemic evil. On the eve of World War II as three branches of Methodism were merging, Dr. Edwin Lewis of Drew Theological Seminary was asked to write a definite theological statement for The Methodist Church. He wrote:

"Much that we once called sin we today call by some other name, but changing the name does not change the dire reality itself. Frustrations, inhibitions, maladjustments, nonsocial attitudes – all these new ways of describing the ancient enemy of human peace and happiness in no way eliminates the enemy. St. Paul defined the gospel as "the power of God unto salvation to everyone who believes." The great task of the Church is to connect God's children with that power. The gospel of Christ can actually save human lives and restore them to God. It can enable the drunk to attain sobriety, change the thief to become an honest citizen, bring home the prodigal son, rehabilitate broken homes, strengthen weak wills, destroy hate in one's spirit, and create peace in troubled breasts. This is not mere verbalism; it is a sober fact of something that has been taking place for centuries and is still happening today." [46]

United Methodist Bishop Scott Jones points out that Wesley clarifies voluntary sins as willful transgressions of the law of God. In this arena of our choices, Wesley includes "inward sins" of tempers, thoughts, lusts, and hate; and our "outward sins" of overt bad behavior. Jones clarifies that Wesley recognizes the inevitability of involuntary sins ("sins of infirmity because they arise either out of our ignorance or our being caught unawares").

Jones then reminds us that sin goes beyond the individual and infects the cultural. The great contribution of the 20th century to the concept of sin was to broaden it to include society's warped values of racism, sexism, the acceptability of

---

46 Op. Cit., Lewis, *The Faith We Declare,* 196-197.

pornography, "dirty jokes," and materialism.[47]

Sin has deeper roots than personal choices. This affects every aspect of our theology. Bishop Kenneth Carder is our teacher here:

> "This disease of the soul – sin – infects all human beings. It invades every aspect of life. Its power exceeds human strength and cannot be defeated by will power. "Demonic forces pervade institutions, individuals, cultures, and systems. We fall victim to their prey without realizing it. The insidious powers of sin and death assault humanity with weapons of deceit, treachery, coercion, manipulation, and violence. The results are the persistent distortion of the divine image in humanity." [48]

Goaded by theologians like Reinhold Niebuhr, United Methodist seminary faculties in the 20th century typically moved sin to the level of societal prejudices, systemic evil, and "tribal" prejudice. Niebuhr documented that individuals can be moral, but no socio-economic system is moral.

Many efforts have been and are being made to remove these injustices that are manifest in "race and clan." Contrary to some voices, "social justice" is biblical. We need to read anew the book of Amos, and Jesus' reading from Isaiah in his local synagogue! (Luke 4:18-21 {NIV}).

Ted Campbell's little *Digest of Methodist Doctrine* sums up our distinctiveness of the Wesleyan "way of salvation":

> "The 'way of salvation' is one of Methodism's spiritual treasures: …{it}seeks comprehensive transformation by God's grace. …we should not only be inspired…as it appeared in the eighteenth century. We should be asking how people experience divine grace today." [49]

---

47 Jones, Scott, *United Methodist Doctrine: The Extreme Center*, Abingdon, 2002, (paraphrase), 153-154,221-240.

48 Carder, Kenneth, *Living Our Own Beliefs*, Discipleship Resources, 2003, 48-49.

49 Op. Cit., Campbell, 62-63.

Let us do a reality check! Sin is personal and cultural. An important dimension of being saved is understanding sin– its persistence, perniciousness, and pervasiveness. Charles Yrigoyen of Drew Theological Seminary has written with wisdom: "This involves all of us. It is the condition in which we live. It manifests itself in all sorts of ways, individually and in the human community. In Wesley's words it is 'unbelief.'" Yrigoyen continues, "There is a price to be paid for living a life of unbelief. When we live apart from God, we live under the power of sin and are denied the full blessing and joy that God intends for each and all of us." [50]

50 Yrigoyen, Charles, *Belief Matters-United Methodism's Doctrinal Standards,* Abingdon, 2001, 24.

Questions for Discussion and Reflection

Do you agree that we need to face up to sin within the context of God's never ending love for us? Think about this in the context of parents and children. When children make a mess of their lives, do we want them to work through the feeling their parents are "out to get them and send them to hell," or rather that their parents will go to the threshold of hell to bring them "home"?

If you want to delve into a little history, compare the philosophy of the Enlightenment in Wesley's day and the philosophy of secular humanism today. Before you respond, read again Edwin Lewis' concern about "changing the name of sin" to "frustrations, inhibitions, maladjustments, and non-social attitudes." (This is a question for "extra credit"!)

Read Steve Harper's quote again–"If sin were 'a thing,' we could escape it but because it is an infection, the only option is healing." Have you ever before seen this distinction between a "clinical" and a "juridical" way of defining sin? One makes God the "Great Physician." The other makes God the "Judge." Where is your comfort zone?

Whether or not you have read William Young's book, *The Shack*, how does the quote in which "Mack" is told that he is experienced in judging grab you?

Did older generations see sin too narrowly? What was the "morality code" prior to World War II? What societal sins were accepted without objection, even from the pulpit?

Does the present emphasis on "social justice" tend to overlook the continuing necessity for "personal holiness"?

Prior to Aldersgate, John Wesley tried to "save himself" by "holiness of heart and life"—living an almost monastic lifestyle. At Aldersgate, he recognized that only a divine "energy" beyond him could assure him of being saved. Wesley called this "experimental divinity." Only as we understand this are we ready for God to save us. Where are you in this journey?

"I abhor the doctrine of predestination.... No Scripture can mean that God is not love, o that his mercy is not over all his works. That is, whatever it prove beside, no Scripture can prove predestination."

John Wesley, 1725

"For if a sick man knows that he must unavoidably die or unavoidably recover, ...it is not reasonable for him to take any (medicine) at all. He might justly say, 'If I am ordained to life, I shall live; if to death, I shall die."

John Wesley, 1725

Our blessed Lord said, "If anyone is thirsty, let him come to me and drink.... Streams of water will flow from within him."

John 7:37, 38b (NIV)

The apostle Paul said to the sophisticated Athenians who worshiped the Olympian gods: 'In the past God overlooked such ignorance, but now he commands all people everywhere to repent.'

Acts 17:30 (NIV)

Thus saith St. Peter: 'The Lord is not slow in keeping his promise, as some understand slowness. He is patient with you, not wanting anyone to perish, but everyone to come to repentance.

II Peter 3:9 (NIV)

"I write this to you so that you will not sin. But if anybody does sin, we have one who speaks to the Father in our defense – Jesus Christ, the Righteous One."

I John 2:1-2 (NIV)

"I urge... that...requests, prayers, intercession, and thanksgiving be made for everyone, for kings and all those in authority....This is good, and pleases God our Savior, who wants all men to be saved and to come to a knowledge of the truth."

I Timothy 2:1-4

"Sent by my Lord, on you I call; the invitation is to all. Come all the world! Come sinner thou! All things in Christ are ready now. Come all ye souls by sin oppressed, ye restless wanderers after rest; ye poor, and maimed, and halt, and blind, in Christ a hearty welcome find. Come this moment at his call and live for him who died for all."

Charles Wesley, 1747

41

Chapter Three

Wesleyans are Arminians, not Calvanists – and Why!

Calvinism dominates the neo-evangelical, "independent church" trend among growing churches in the 21st century. Time magazine ranked Calvinism third in its list of the "Top 10" forces changing the postmodern world. Most Christians in the Calvinist denominations have heard a lot about Calvin, and know a lot about his doctrines. On the other hand, most Christians who are theological progeny of Jacob Arminius do not use the term "Arminian" to describe their Christian doctrine.

One reason that Calvinism is better known is that John Calvin was an attorney who wrote a systematic theology based on the theological premise that God is all powerful. Since God is all powerful, Calvin concluded that God remains in total control of all creation – natural and human. From that logic, it is a short step to believing that God preordains the eternal destiny of every person. So, Calvin concluded, God elects some humans to be saved because God is merciful, but as a matter of justice, allows the rest of humankind to receive our just desserts – damnation. Even people who think that all of us can be saved have "Calvinist" sayings like, "We all have a time to die," or that every death is God's will, even if free choices have shortened life with bad habits.

Who was "Arminius"?

Jacob Arminius was a child prodigy adopted by a Catholic priest. Recognizing Arminius as a prodigy, the priest sent him to school in Utrecht, The Netherlands. When the priest died,

43

a Lutheran professor took the brilliant boy to Marlburg to a
Protestant school. He lost all his family in the bloody, religious
"Thirty Years' War." Homeless and totally dispirited, he found
refuge in the home of a Dutch Reformed pastor who sent him
to the University of Leiden, a school espousing Calvinism. He
earned distinction as a scholar and became a pastor and professor in the Dutch Reformed Church. In due season, they sent him
for graduate work in Geneva to study under the great Professor Theodore Beza, the man who followed Calvin as the most
preeminent teacher of the Reformed tradition.

While studying and teaching in Geneva, Arminius became
disenchanted with one Calvinist doctrine – predestination.
He became convinced that the persons who are saved are not
predetermined by God's will but volitionally determined by our
faith in God's grace. He came to believe that Jesus died for all
persons, not just the Elect. He came back to The Netherlands
in 1588, married, had several children and served as pastor of
the Dutch Reformed Church in Amsterdam. His popularity as
a preacher made the church grow phenomenally. Like Jesus,
"The common people heard him gladly."

He became a full professor at the University of Leiden in
1603. However, the rigid Calvinists treated him shamefully
and he was scheduled for trial when he died from his chronic
asthma or tuberculosis. After his early death in 1649, he was
tried and convicted of heresy by his peers, but his doctrine
lived on. John Wesley became an Arminian and from 1777 until
his death, Wesley published "The Arminian Magazine" that
was read by almost every literate Methodist. Therefore, the official position of all branches of Methodism is "Arminianism."

Calvin came logically to his theory that God predestines
every person to be saved or lost. The words "predestinate" or
"predestinated" are mentioned only four times in the Bible, but
Calvin based his entire doctrine on the words, "For those God
foreknew he also predestined .... And those whom he predestined, he also called, he also justified; those he justified, he also
glorified" (Romans 8:29a, 30 (NIV)). Arminius saw a conflict between

Calvin's view of being pre-determined or pre-destined in birth, disease, accidents, death, and eternal salvation or damnation on the one hand, and human action which causes births and accidents and many diseases and deaths. That is why Arminius questioned his own church leaders.

John Wesley was a member of an Oxford college faculty; he taught logic, but had decided in college that predestination makes God the author of the bad things that happen to good people. However, unlike Calvin, his beliefs and values were not developed into a systematic theology, per se. Wesley's sermons were consistent in the same invitation that Jesus gave, "... whoever comes to me I will never drive away." (John 6:37 (NIV)) Calvin, Arminius, and Wesley all believed in God's absolute sovereignty, and that we are saved only by God's grace.

Many Christians might well read the foregoing paragraphs, wave their hand, and ask, "Who cares?" But the wisdom of an examined life far outweighs the wisdom of an unexamined life. Doctrine does matter.

If We Are Arminians, What Is It that We Believe?

Mildred Bangs Wynkoop and her brother, Carl Bangs, were probably the most thorough and articulate representatives of Wesleyan Arminianism in the twentieth century. Wynkoop taught at Central Nazarene Theological Seminary in Kansas City. She gave us this insight. Arminius rejected the predestination concept of God's power because:

Scripture's portrait of God is more about God's love than God's control. The essence of the Gospel is John 3:16 – 'God so loved that God gave....'

Predestination was not adopted by any of the Ecumenical Councils that established official Catholic orthodoxy.

Predestination makes God responsible for our sins and makes us as robots.

45

Predestination insists that God elects or condemns a person as we are conceived in our mother's womb and before there is any temptable conscience.

Dr. Wynkoop explained Arminius' and Wesley's "good news" this way:

Wesleyanism is Arminian orthodoxy infused with the warmth and power of the Holy Spirit. Arminius saw only dimly what Wesley saw clearly. Both were dominated by the Word of God, and in that respect became our proper forebears in that they grounded their theology in Scripture, not philosophy. Wesley's emphasis was not on free will, as is often misstated, but it is on free grace granted to any and all men and accounting for all the good found in the world. Natural man is devilish, corrupt, evil. "The human person is still human; a weak, fallible, temptable being. Only with a continuing fresh supply of grace through the Holy Spirit can this humanness be suppressed. [51]

Arminius believed in the sovereignty and omnipotence of God as much as Calvin or Augustine did. Since all humanity has fallen to the power of sin, grace is absolutely necessary for redemption, another point at which he was in agreement with his Reformed Dutch tradition. However, in contrast to their prioritization of God's power, Arminius prioritized God's grace as the ground of God's being.

For Arminius, God's love trumps God's power; therefore God limits his power of predestining a few for salvation, and allows every person the liberty of embracing God's grace or resisting it. To Arminius, "God sent his only Son that none should perish, but that all should have eternal life" (John 3:16 {NIV}, paraphrase).

Arminius disagreed with Calvin on two basic points:

---

51 Wynkoop, Mildred Bangs, *Foundations of Wesleyan-Arminian Theology,* Beacon Hill Press, 1967, 68-69.

He believed that Jesus' atonement was unlimited – that it was for all. We all are "elected" to be saved; salvation is conditioned not upon God's favoritism but upon our responding positively to God's amazing grace.

He believed that grace is resistible; we can reject God's love just as we can reject the love of another human being. Love, by definition is synergistic, or cooperant.[52]

To summarize, Arminius believed that the foundation of salvation is seen in God's creating us in God's own image, as we read in Genesis 1:27. With Augustine and Calvin, he believed in original sin which was not predestined but the result of the seduction of temptation. In the rest of the Bible and the rest of human history, we see humanity as Paul described us: "All have fallen short of the glory of God." (Romans 3:23 {NIV})

Consequently and subsequently, we can be saved only by grace as the essential necessity of salvation but that God's grace is universally "ours as a gift from our Maker." Arminius' best biographer, Carl Bangs, a Methodist and a one-time faculty colleague of this writer, called him a "theologian of grace." Our belief is not in a doctrine, per se, but is our faith that we are saved by and in God's grace.

In a Nutshell How Does Calvinism Define Itself?

Jacob Arminius died in 1609 after the religious authorities in The Netherlands removed him from his pulpit. Posthumously, he was tried at the Council of Dort in The Netherlands in 1618. There, Calvinism was summarized in an acronym, the English version of which is still used:

---

52 Op. Cit., Stanglin and McCall, *Jacob Arminius,* Oxford, 2012, 21-22.

Total depravity,

Unconditional election,

Limited atonement,

Irresistible grace,

Perseverance of the saints

The acronym **T.U.L.I.P.** might be a bit simplistic but it was a convenient way to remember a synopsis of Calvin's "plan of salvation." John Piper and other Calvinists have developed what they call "conditional predestination," but that is mostly to win arguments on college campuses and new "church plants." In reality, we must listen also to Glenn Hinson, a moderate Baptist who was once on the faculty of Southern Baptist Seminary. Dr. Hinson has said of contemporary Fundamentalism, "Fundamentalism of a more sophisticated sort traces its roots to Dort Calvinism. Albert Mohler, Jr, President of Southern Baptist Seminary has been called by Time magazine, "the reigning intellectual of the evangelical movement in the U.S." He is described as a "cerebral, churchy...five point Calvinist" referring to the five points of the "Dort Calvinist" T.U.L.I.P." We who are Arminian need to know what the five foundational points of Calvinism are, and that indeed the nature of God is at stake!

"Total Depravity" Both Augustine and Calvin believed that humanity is so totally depraved that we cannot turn to God for salvation. God must come to us, that is, "elect" us to be saved. Salvation then is "monergistic" with only God as the operative.

We agree that the heart of the human problem is the problem of the human heart. Theologian Albert Outler says that from the image of God in which we were created, "Something has gone fearfully awry in the human enterprise." Outler once wrote euphemistically that "We believe in total depravity, but not in tee-total depravity!" That is, Calvinists insist that as persons addicted to sin and estranged from God since birth, no one of us can, in Jesus' words regarding the prodigal son "come to himself." We cannot be a seeker or pray the prayer of a repenting sinner, but must be chosen, elected, saved by God's elective grace. That is "tee-total" depravity.

"Unconditional Election" The "U" in the acronym "T.U.L.I.P" means that God unconditionally elects us to be saved. That is, we have no role in our salvation. The favorite Scripture for this aspect of Calvinism is, "Those whom he predestined, he called" (Romans 8:30 {NIV}). This means that we are not elected to be saved on the basis of the life we have chosen to live, but on the basis of God's predestined sovereignty when we were conceived.

"Limited Atonement" The "L" in the T.U.L.I.P. acronym might shock you! It means that Jesus did not die for everyone; his atoning grace was limited for the predestined Elect. According to Jacob Arminius, to be elected at conception could mean that persons who live a life of disobedience to God, dissipation of their body, moral turpitude, abusive relationships, and criminal behavior would still be among the Elect while the person living a good life would be preemptively condemned. This, again according to Arminius, is virtually a false doctrine.[53]

"Irresistible Grace" The "I" in the T.U.L.I.P. acronym is baffling! It means that if God has elected you to be saved, you cannot resist God's saving grace. No matter what you do with your life, you cannot resist God's sovereign control over your eternal destiny. Some critics of Reformed faith communities have asked why anyone should be motivated to live a good life if you never knew whether you were elected to be saved or damned. After all, even reprobates might well be predestined to be saved! The response of those same critics is that in communities like the Puritans of Massachusetts Bay Colony, your motivation to have "clean hands and a pure heart" was that in the hope you were one of the Elect, you should act like it!

---

53 Ibid. 129.

"Perseverance of the Saints" The "P" in the acronym T.U.L.I.P. means, in street language, "once saved, always saved." In former generations it was called "eternal security." Calvinism asserts a static relationship in which we cannot backslide. Considering the record of human behavior, we beg to differ. However, "eternal security" is a foolproof argument in that if a person who is seen by all to be a Christian suddenly develops a lifestyle or does some dastardly deed contrary to a Christian's life, you could simply say, "That proves he was never saved."

We Arminians disagree with each letter! Just as we need to know what Calvinists mean by the T.U.L.I.P. We need to know why we find Calvinism contrary to the macroview of Scripture.

We confess original sin as the natural spiritual state of every person. As Frank Sinatra crooned, we all sing, "I'll Do It My Way." We are fallen from our creation, and all of us are sinners, but we are not so totally depraved that we cannot sense God's "whispers to our inner soul."

The Current Popularity of Calvinism

In 2009, the 500th birth year of John Calvin, "Christianity Today" magazine had his picture on the front cover with the headline, "John Calvin: The Comeback Kid." The magazine is correct. In the nineteenth century's revival preaching to the masses, Arminianism's invitation to people with broken lives prevailed on the frontier. However, in the twenty-first century, Calvinism's invitation is for people to believe that if they "stay on plan," God will work everything out for them.

Rick Warren popularized Calvinist theology in his bestseller, *The Purpose Driven Life.* His chapter two defines his belief in predestination:

"Your parents may not have planned you, but God did. Long before you were conceived by your parents, you were conceived in the mind of God. God custom made your body just the way he wanted it. Many children are unplanned by their parents, but they are not unplanned by God. Your parents had just the DNA that God wanted to make you. He planned the days of your life in advance, choosing the exact time of your birth and death." [54]

Warren, a graduate of Dallas Theological Seminary, is in this passage teaching what is called "monergism." "Mono" means one; monergism teaches that God and only God is in total control of all that happens in every human event. This, in effect, makes humans sheer robots, created to do what the Creator/Designer controls, in life, in death, and in life after death.

Multiple millions have found spiritual comfort and life purpose in reading Warren's book, but it means we cannot question God and retain our faith in Him as Heavenly Father. When life gets irrationally "out of balance," most people do not like to ascribe to God all the bad things that happen to good people. Indeed, when Dr. Warren's wife developed cancer and their son committed suicide, he admitted on national television that he did not lay the fault of his wife's disease or their son's death to God. Rigid predestination does what John Wesley's mother wrote to him when he was in college:" "It makes God the author of evil."

In William Young's novel *The Shack*, "Mack's" little girl is murdered. Mack accuses God of being responsible for a serial killer murdering several children. God responds in a way that Wesley and Arminius would:

"Don't ever assume that my using something for good means that I caused it or that I need it to accomplish my purposes. Just because I work incredible good out of unspeakable tragedies doesn't mean I orchestrate the tragedies. Grace does not depend on suffering to exist, but where there is suffering, you will find grace." [55]

A favorite verse of Scripture is often translated with the

---

54 Warren, Rick, *The Purpose Driven Life*, Zondervan, 2002, 22-26.

55 Op. Cit., Young, 26.

wrong Greek grammar! "All things work together for good for them who love God" is not grammatically correct and is therefore theologically wrong. The verse should have "God" as the subject rather than "All things." It should read, "We know that in all things God works for the good of those who love him..." (Romans 8:28 (NIV)). If we just pause and think about it, many people would be bitter toward God if our faith depended on "all things working for good..."

Wesleyan Arminianism

Let us remember that Calvin and Arminius were both tenured university professors and that Wesley was a faculty member of Lincoln College of Oxford University. He could have remained at Oxford, but he reluctantly left both the university and the pulpit to begin a ministry "where the people were." After 1738, he became a traveling preacher and shaped his theology on the fly. He was first a missionary in Georgia. Then he preached at the shafts of the mines, the gates of the factories, and the doors of the pubs. He had a heart for the common person and wanted "none to be left behind." He preached to the "leftovers and has-beens" of English society. Albert Outler correctly identified Wesley as a "folk theologian."

Wesley was a true scholar and Methodism's theology comes from "the light of many lamps." The theology of John Wesley was not purely Arminian. It also reflected his deep reading in Catholic saints, Eastern Orthodox theologians, Anglican Puritan piety, Moravian quietism, Dutch Arminianism, and in Enlightenment philosophers such as Adam Smith, David Hume, John Locke, Isaac Newton, and Frenchmen like Montesquieu. Don Thorsen, a Pentecostal, has created an Arminian acronym that is Wesleyan to the point that all of Wesley's legacy might consider teaching it – A.C.U.R.A: [56]

---

56 Op. Cit., Thorsen.

All are fallen from our original state of righteousness and are sinful

Conditional election is not conditional on God's election but on our response to God's amazing grace

Unlimited atonement is so obvious – Jesus died for all, not just some

Resistible grace is the byproduct of God's giving us the liberty of choice – free will

Assurance of salvation is the witness of the Spirit that confirms our being forgiven

Arminianism is the antecedent of Methodist grace theology. According to Wesley scholar Richard Heitzenrater of Duke Divinity School, Wesley decided to meet the Calvinist challenge head-on in November 1777 by producing a monthly magazine himself – "The Arminian Magazine." Through that medium, Wesley popularized the work of Jacob Arminius. Heitzenrater says Wesley knew Arminianism would offend some, but "was confident that ninety-nine in a hundred persons in England rejected absolute predestination and would thus not take offence."

In his sermon, "The Image of God," on Genesis 1:27, John Wesley preached, "Man not only sprung from God, but the image of his divine Parent was still visible. He had the capacity of distinguishing truth from falsehood. Man had the liberty to keep or to change his first estate – a will to make choices." (Wesley called this God's "political image." In another place, Wesley had the temerity to call this *Imago Dei* "original righteousness.") This is a far cry from anything remotely Calvinistic.

Indeed, Wesley insisted that we can still hear the whispers of God's spirit. This is affirmed in the conventional wisdom that we have a conscience, an innate nudge of what is right. In St. Paul's words, "God's Spirit touches our spirits and confirms who we really are. We know who he is and who we are – Father and children." (Romans 8:28 {The Message})

God's love is a "hound of heaven" who is seeking love. If we listen to our soul at the "God moments" of our lives, we can "hear" the "still small voice" of God calling us. Every spiritual nudge from the church to ICU, to a hiking trail, to a night of insomnia is based on the premise that we can "hear our Savior calling." Every "God moment" is Jesus' "tenderly calling today," and is predicated on following our hearts to say, "Yes" to the call of the Spirit. Election is conditional not upon God's capricious favoritism, but to our positive response.

We repeat here words of wisdom from Mildred Bangs Wynkoop:

> "Wesley infused Armianism with the warmth and power of the Holy Spirit." [57] Wesley built his theology upon a dynamic understanding of the ongoing presence of God's Holy Spirit interfacing with our human spirit in the ups and downs of living through changing times and the seasons of our lives.[58] Wesley insisted that God's attribute of love trumps his attribute of omnipotent power; therefore, his power was conditioned by love for all humanity. Election was not for "the chosen" but for every human being. "Wesley's emphasis was not so much on free will as on free grace, granted to any and to all." [59]

God's love could, and would, and does forgive in every extremity of human thought, word, and deed. "Behind" creation and infused into every phase and facet of creation is the personal love of a personal God that we call "grace." Original grace preceded original sin. Grace is not received as "Step one, step two, and step three." Grace flows as God's whispers to our soul – a God-initiated "voice" from the baby's first cry

---

57 Op. Cit., Wynkoop 68.

58 Op. Cit., Thorsen, xv (paraphrased).

59 Op. Cit., Wynkoop, 69.

to the "death rattle" of our last breaths. As George Matheson, the blind Scottish Presbyterian preacher, put it, God's is truly a "love that will not let me go. I trace the rainbow through the rain and feel the promise is not vain."

Methodists sing as one of their favorite hymns the words of Charles Wesley: "Jesus, thou art all compassion, pure, unbounded love thou art, visit us with thy salvation, enter every trembling heart." If Jesus is "all compassion" whose desire is to "enter every trembling heart", then Jacob Arminius and John Wesley were right and John Calvin was wrong!

We Methodists insist that "Vital to any proper understanding of God is an understanding of God's love." [60] This is a basic Christian question because at some time, we all ask, "Did Jesus really die for every single person who ever lived?" Does God really show no partiality? (Acts 10:34-35 {The Message}). Does God's mercy really trump his sense of justice? We trust this chapter has helped you do your homework on whether you are a follower of John Calvin or Jacob Arminius and John Wesley!

Wesley asks the tough question, "But is this grace free for all?" Calling into question the Calvinist position of Christ's "limited atonement," Wesley then defines what he sees as the essence of Calvinism: "By virtue of an eternal, unchangeable, irresistible decree of God, one part of mankind is infallibly saved and the rest infallibly damned; it being impossible that any of the former should be damned or that any of the latter should be saved." Then he concludes, "If this be so, all preaching is in vain."

He calls predestination "a flat contradiction, not only to the whole scope and tenor of Scripture, but also to those particular texts which expressly declare, 'God is love.'" Wesley's emphasis was more on "free grace to all and in all" than it was on humankind's "free will." He quotes Psalm 145:9: "The Lord is good to all; he has compassion on all he has made...." He refers to God's revelation to Peter that "God shows no partiality" as Peter was called to preach to Cornelius.

---

60 Op. Cit., Stanglin, 126.

Then Wesley rolls out a litany of scriptural references to Jesus' death for "all," for "every man," for the "whole world." He refers to Jesus' invitation, "Come to me all you who labor and are heavy laden, and I will give you rest." He says if that weren't true, all references to God's weeping would be "crocodile tears, weeping over the prey which were doomed for destruction."

The Wesleyan fundamental doctrine, then, is that God is inherently love, mercy, and grace. Wesley's sermon, "Free Grace," preached in 1739 at Bristol, was published to refute Calvinism. It begins, "How freely does God love the world! While we were yet sinners, 'Christ died for the ungodly and how freely with him does he 'give us all things!' The grace or love of God, whence cometh our salvation, is free in all and free for all."

Charles Wesley wrote this doctrine into many hymns, one of which is "Come sinners to the gospel feast; let every soul be Jesus' guest. Ye need not one be left behind, for God hath bid all humankind." Jesus said it plainly, "Whoever comes to me I will never drive away." (John 6:37 {NIV}) Grace is the divine initiative and is to all; faith is the human response of those who volitionally walk through God's threshold of grace. God's role in salvation is that the Holy Spirit knocks; our role is that we choose to open or not to open (Revelation 3:20 {NIV}).

Arminianism is not based on justice, but on love. Since the divine operative is grace, we are all welcomed home by a waiting father, just as the "prodigal son" was. That was the controversy in Wesley's day; that is the controversy in the 21st century. The question boils down to this: "Is the nature of God inherently justice or inherently love?" Acknowledging that the Calvinists have their own scriptural proof texts, Wesley adroitly admits that he does not know the full meaning of texts like "God hardened Pharaoh's heart." Then he adds:

"There are many Scriptures the true sense whereof neither you nor I shall know till death is swallowed up in victory. But this I know, better it were to say it had no sense at all than to say it had such a sense as this. It cannot mean, whatever is meant besides, that the God of truth is a liar. No Scripture can mean that God is not love, or that his mercy is not over all his works. This is the blasphemy for which (however much I love the people who assert it), I abhor the doctrine of predestination."

Randy Maddox adds to that,

"The character of God and God's mode of relating to human beings was always at stake in Arminius' debates with the Calvinists. He insisted that God was not a despot who arbitrarily chose some for life and others for death. God's relation to humanity was expressed in Jesus Christ; 'Whosoever will may come' was the repeated theme." [61]

Jerry Walls and Joseph Dongell created a novel piece of fiction that provides a picture of the God-initiated dimension of prevenient grace, in contrast to Calvinism's concept of elective grace.[62] They picture a prisoner held by terrorists for a long time in a dank cell. She has succumbed to the "Stockholm syndrome" and identified with her captors to the point that she makes no attempt to escape. Only an invasion from outside will rescue her.

The Calvinist view of divine invasion is simple: God invades the camp, swoops up the prisoner, strips off her shackles and blindfold, and makes her free, even though she does not want freedom. The rescuer is irresistible; she is freed against her will. God has been the lone actor throughout. The Arminian view of the same scenario is different: God steals into the prison and makes it to the bedside of the prisoner. God begins to whisper, "Do you know who you are? Let me tell you. Here is a picture of you before you were captured. Do you know what has happened to you as your captors have made you feel at home in this dark, dank cell? You are not theirs; you are mine

---

61 Maddox, Randy, *Rethinking Wesley's Theology,* Kingswood, 1998, 39.

62 Walls, Jerry, and Dongell, *Why I Am Not A Calvinist,* IVP, 2004 69.

and I have come to take you home." Truth begins to dawn. The Savior holds up a mirror and shines a light in it and she sees her sunken eyes and matted hair and frail body. He says, "Do you see what they have done to you? You are not theirs; you are your parents' daughter."

The Rescuer presses on. "I know a part of you suspects that I have come to harm you, but let me show you my hands. See this blood? I crawled through an awful tangle of barbed wire to get to you. I want to carry you out of here right now. Trust me. Put your arm around my neck and surrender yourself to me as we get to freedom." She could say, "No," but she responds to this seeking, rescuing care, puts her arm around his neck, and welcomes being carried from captivity to freedom. The story gives a fictionalized version of God's "whisper" to us in our human situation! Her voluntary decision to come with her rescuer is the Arminian concept of being saved.

This little drama portrays so well that we have been captured by sin and developed a comfort zone in our imprisonment. God seeks us out, whispers in our soul, and awakens us to the reality of our circumstances. Like the prodigal son who "came to himself," we do not resist rescue from bondage. We voluntarily walk through the threshold of grace.

The reason we Arminians insist on some measure of free will is that we do not see persons as marionettes on the end of a string pulled from above the stage! Nor do we see ourselves as robots pre-programmed for involuntary tasks (or words!). Rather we have the freedom to accept God's love or reject God's love.

Randy Maddox at Duke Divinity School calls it "responsible grace." God nudges; we respond. Maddox also calls it "synergistic grace." Jesus calls us to be "in sync" with God's love. Mildred Bangs Wynkoop has written, "Being a Christian means having a faith which is active in love. Faith is not static, but dynamic; it is a relationship. For Wesley "faith" could not save anyone, but "faith in Christ" could because our faith in God's grace demonstrated in Christ is verbalized as "What a Friend we have in Jesus."

Questions for Discussion and Reflection

Was the word "Arminian" new to you? If not, where had you seen or heard about it before?

Do you agree with Susanna Wesley's distinction between God's "foreknowledge" and God's "predestination" of all events?

Were you acquainted with the acronym "T.U.L.I.P." which continues to be used by Calvinists to summarize their doctrine? Which "letter," if any, "turns you off" to what you believe about God, the work of Christ, and our ability to resist grace?

Were you acquainted with the acronym "A.C.U.R.A.?" Probably not! Is it meaningful to you in defining your own theology?

Do you believe it is possible for a person to be truly saved and then to backslide? If so, you are an Arminian!

Was this chapter helpful in defining God's grace as "for all and in all?"

As the chapter unfolded, did you find yourself in agreement or disagreement with Arminianism?

Which passages of Scripture from this chapter will you underline in your Bible?

Having read the chapter, do you consider Wesleyan Arminianism or Calvinism to be more reflective of Jesus? Of Paul's letters? Or your personal faith?

Gratitude is our response to realizing that God loves us. "In the numerous expressions of God's love on our behalf lie the strongest claim to our gratitude. Every reasonable person is to love God because God's power, his wisdom, yea, and his goodness are infinite. 'We love Him, says the Apostle John, 'because He first loved us.'"

Paraphrase from Wesley's sermon "The Love of God"

"Because they are children of God...they continually look up to God as their reconciling and loving Father {to whom} they cry for daily bread...."

From sermon "The Marks of the New Birth" 1748

"God is Love. Whoever lives in love lives in God and God in him."

I John 4:16

"The darling attribute I praise which all alike may prove, The glory of thy boundless grace, Thy universal love."

"Jesus, thou art all compassion, pure unbounded love thou art; Visit us with thy salvation, enter every trembling heart."

Charles Wesley

Chapter Four

Good News! John 3:16 is the Gist of the Gospel

"God so loved the ..."

"Wesley was clear about the nature and problem of sin. It disrupts and damages our relationship with God and our neighbors; it creates havoc. But Wesley was not preoccupied with sin. While the sinful state and its results is bad news, it is overshadowed by the good news of God's action in Christ to reconcile, heal, and create in us a new life." [63]

The Foundation of Salvation is Not Our Faith, but God's Love

Much bad theology begins with the human situation, but the first word in "the way of salvation" is not about us at all. The first word is about God! The character of God is love. In the year 1050 Meir Ben Isaac Nehorai wrote in Aramaic these words:

"Could we with ink the ocean fill, and were the skies of parchment made

Were every stalk on earth a quill, and every man a scribe by trade

To write the love of God above would drain the ocean dry

Nor could the scroll contain the whole though stretched from sky to sky.

---

63 Op. Cit., 25.

O love of God, how rich and pure! How measureless and strong!

It shall forevermore endure the saints and angels' song." [64]

Over and over again, Wesley insisted that John 3:16 is foundational, and he placed this verse in tandem with I John 4:9-10 that reads, "This is how God showed his love among us: He sent his one and only Son into the world that we might live through him. This is love: not that we loved God, but that he loved us and sent his Son as an atoning sacrifice for our sins." [65] A few sentences further John the Elder reminds us, "We love because He first loved us." (I John 4:19 {NIV}) Albert Outler has taught us well in saying:

The Christian gospel for our being made guiltless is not that Christ appeased the Father's wrath; rather, he is the agent of the Father's redemptive compassion. We actually can participate in God's love in Christ through the Holy Spirit. The good news is that God is indeed the giver of life's meanings and joys and hopes, that life in his love is ultimately secure and can even now be serene.... This potential inspired Paul to write, 'What then can separate us from the love of Christ?' [66]

Bishop Scott Jones cites Wesley's sermon, *The Way to the Kingdom:*

"The substance of all is this, 'Jesus Christ came into the world to save sinners,' or 'God loved the world so much that he gave his only begotten Son, to the end we might not perish, but have eternal life." (John 3:16 {NIV}) Importantly, John continues, 'Indeed, God did not send the Son into the world to condemn the world, but in order that the world might be saved through him.'" [67]

---

64 Internet.

65 Op. Cit., Jones, Scott, 107.

66 Outler, Albert, *Theology in the Wesleyan Spirit,* Discipleship Resources, 1974, 65.

67 Op. Cit., Wesley, Sermon, *The Way to the Kingdom,* Outler, ed., Vol 1, 229.

We must note that John 3:16 follows immediately after Jesus' conversation with Nicodemus. In John 3:3 Jesus used a Greek word that has two meanings: "from above" and "again." Nicodemus misunderstood Jesus because he heard "again" when Jesus meant "from above." (NRSV, NIV footnote). Then, our beloved old King James Version was incorrect in its translation of the last phrase of John 3:16 as "everlasting life." Most all recent translations use the correct term, "eternal life." There is a vast difference! "Everlasting life" simply means infinite chronology – on and on forever. "Eternal life" is a qualitative life change that comes with conversion. It is a synonym for what Jesus promised in John 10:10 as "abundant life." We see the same word in 3:36 and 17:3.

In I John 4-8, we find the Bible's only formal definition of God: "God is love." In his Explanatory Notes Upon the New Testament, Wesley's comments on that text are noteworthy:

This little sentence brought St. John more sweetness, even in the time he was writing it, than the whole world can bring. God is often styled holy, righteous, wise, but describing Him as love intimates that this is His darling, His reigning attribute, the attribute that sheds an amiable glory on all His own perfections.[68]

I John 4:19 reads, "We love Him because He first loved us." In his commentary on that verse, Wesley wrote, "This is the sum of all religion, the genuine model of Christianity. None can say more. Why then should they say less, or less intelligibly?" [69]

In John Wesley's "Sermon on the Mount VI," he says of the opening line in the Lord's Prayer, "If he is a Father, then he is good, then he is loving to his children." He describes God as "our Father who day by day sustains the life he has given; whose continuing love we know, and who every moment receives life and breath and all things. So much more boldly let us come to him, and 'we shall find mercy and grace to help in time of need.'" (Hebrews 4:16 {NIV}) We pray because we love and because we are loved by our heavenly Father.

---

68 Wesley, John, *Explanatory Notes Upon the New Testament*, Epworth, 914.

69 Ibid, 915.

God's love is neither elective nor selective; it is for all. Wesley's central thrust refers to Jesus' words, "Let anyone who is thirsty come to me, and let the one who believes in me drink."(John 7:37 {NIV}) This is reminiscent of Isaiah 55:1, "Come, all you who are thirsty, come to the waters; and you who have no money, come, buy and eat! Come, buy wine and milk without money and without cost." Isaiah continues in verse 3, "Give ear and come to me; hear me, that your soul may live."

Bishop Scott Jones summed up the centrality of Wesley's grace theology: "For Wesley, grace is the manifestation of God's love." [70] He loved one of the latest written of all New Testament verses, "The Lord is not wanting anyone to perish, but everyone to come to repentance." (II Peter 3:9 {NIV}) A contemporary gospel song personalizes this love with these lyrics:

"He knew me yet He loved me; when He was on the cross, I was on His mind."

Charles Wesley also expresses this in his invitational hymn:

"Come sinners to the gospel feast, let every soul be Jesus' guest. Ye need not one be left behind for God hath bid all humankind." [71]

Rick Warren sounds like an Arminian when he writes, "God wants us to run to him, not from him." In his own dark night of wondering why his wife had cancer and their son died, Rick Warren searched the Scriptures anew and found that 365 times in the Bible, "God says, 'Don't be afraid.' That's one 'Fear not' for every day of the year!" [72]

---

70 Op. Cit., Jones, 107.

71 Wesley, Charles, *The United Methodist Hymnal*, Abingdon, 1989, Hymn No. 339.

72 Warren, Rick, *The Purpose of Christmas*, Howard Books, 2005, 30.

Becoming and Being a Christian is a Relationship, not a Plan

The heritage of the revival, the "Decisions for Christ" of the Billy Graham Crusades, and the evangelistic methods of campus groups like Young Life, CRU, Fellowship of Christian Athletes, Intervarsity Fellowship, and other approaches are bringing about an immediate conversion experience. Most of them utilized a series of questions that led from one's confession as a sinner, to repentance, to affirmative answers regarding belief in the Bible as the Word of God, Jesus' dying on the cross to save us, and our accepting Christ as our personal savior. There is nothing inherently wrong with any of these questions and millions have come to Christ through some variant of this methodology.

There are some shortcomings in the typical "Q & A" means to bringing people to Christ as Savior. First of all, they tend to be "cookie-cutter" in their questions and required answers. They allow no space for encouraging the seeker to share her or his journey, however unusual or dysfunctional it might have been. The "counselor" has been trained in a lockstep "one size must fit all" process. Secondly, little preparation is made for the letdown once the new convert is out of the emotional and supportive "groupthink" of the Christian band of brothers and sisters. We don't say enough about it, but Wesley had a "dark night of the soul" in which he doubted the confidence he experienced at Aldersgate. Shortly after a new conversion, the bottom can fall out of a person's life with trauma, tragedy, or yielding quickly to an old addiction. Thirdly, there is the issue of terminology, "God's Plan of Salvation."

Millions of tracts have been distributed with what Fundamentalists call "God's Plan of Salvation." However, Wesleyans do not prefer the term, "Plan of Salvation." The word "plan" is out of corporate culture, often modified by "business plan" or "strategic plan." Wesley, Latin student that he was, preferred the term *"via salutis"* which translates, "way of salvation." See the difference? The word "way" implies "journey" or "walk." To Wesley, salvation was relational, like a parent and child, a married couple, a professor and student, or two friends. Wise parents don't have a plan for their children; they have a relationship. If parents have a plan for rearing children, they are in for a rude awakening! Plans subject children to goals for success. They create stress for the children and conflicts in the parent-child relationship. By the same token, the dynamics of friendships and marriages are not "plans." They are relationships and they change as our seasons of life change. In friendships, one might move away, or change marital status, or develop a lifestyle that is not conducive to maintaining the friendship. As people tell of their courtships, some moved from acquaintance to friendship to marriage through a long chapter of shared experiences. Others "fall in love" almost immediately upon meeting.

In any relationship, we can either become closer as we soldier on through life or we can drift apart as our lives take differing directions. Becoming a Christian is no different; it might happen almost instantaneously, but most often happens gradually.

Seeing our salvation as a relationship with God recognizes the reality that "being saved" is not so much the adoption of a fixed doctrinal formula or emotional feelings. Being a Christian is essentially a relationship. The African Christians all encourage new converts to seek a friend and ask, "Will you walk with me?" Jesus said, "You are my friends... ." (John 15:14a {NIV}) As a child in a small rural Methodist Church, I remember how meaningful a favorite gospel hymn was to me after my father died:

"What a friend we have in Jesus, all our sins and griefs to bear...,
What a peace we often forfeit, oh, what needless pain we bear...
Can we find a friend so faithful who will all our sorrows share?...
Are we weak and heavy laden, cumbered with a load of care?...
Do thy friends despise, forsake thee?

*...In his arms he'll take and shield thee; thou wilt find a
solace there."*

Our walk with God is very personal and varied. Children
of Christian parents are taken to Sunday School from birth,
taught Christian "courses" or songs as children, taught Bible
verses, taught to say nightly prayers and table grace, and taught
to be morally "good" and ethically "honest." This was the story
of John Wesley's childhood. It is the story of my own childhood.
The parental "playbook" of a Christian mother and father is
Proverbs 22:6, "Train a child in the way he should go, and when
he is old, he will not turn from it." Another is Proverbs 3:6, "In
all your ways acknowledge Him and He will make your paths
straight." Still another that I remember from my mother's
teachings is Proverbs 7:1-3, "My son, keep my words and store
up my commands within you; keep my commands and you will
live; guard my teachings as the apple of your eye. Bind them on
your fingers, write them on the tablet of your heart."

To young Timothy, Paul wrote, "I have been reminded of
your sincere faith, which first lived in your grandmother Lois,
and in your mother Eunice and, I am persuaded, now lives in
you also." (II Timothy 1:5 {NIV})

John Wesley's Journey of Salvation

In John Wesley's life, this parental influence and some
books he read in college led him to the conviction that being a
Christian meant what he called "holy living." In that period of
his life, he wrote about the influence of Jeremy Taylor's book,
Holy Living and Holy Dying: "Instantly I resolved to dedicate
all of my life to God, all my thoughts, and words, and actions."

This would equate any momentary testimony of being
saved; he had all the "answers" right! Yet as we know, he
still lacked the assurance of his salvation, the "witness of the
Spirit," the peace of what Whittier called "the still, small voice
of calm."

Wesley was a holy man long before he was a happy man.
Some people insist that John Wesley became a Christian one

spring evening in May of 1738 on Aldersgate Street in London when he "felt my heart strangely warmed." But that was the culmination of a long journey, and a journey not then ended. Let's look at Wesley's journey.

Wesley's Spiritual Journey

John Wesley was reared in a devoutly Christian home, had no season of his young life when he "sowed wild oats," went to Christ College at Oxford University, and was ordained a priest in the Church of England when he was twenty-three years old. When John Wesley was thirty-two, he had been a college professor in religious studies for six years, had assisted his father as a parish priest for over a year, and had led "The Holy Club" at Oxford.

In 1735 two monumental things happened in his life. First of all, his father died. Samuel Wesley had been stern and strict and rigid, but on his death bed, he said to his sons, "The inward witness, my sons, the inward witness. This is the greatest proof of Christianity." Secondly, only four months after their father's death, both John and Charles Wesley were invited to accompany General Oglethorpe to the colony of Georgia. With their mother's blessing, they accepted. On board the ship there were fifty-nine Moravians from Germany. During the last of three storms at sea, the main mast broke and threatened to capsize the ship.

John Wesley, dedicated to "holy living and holy dying," was afraid to die! Meanwhile, the Moravians were singing hymns and totally at peace. He wanted what the Moravians had! He did not become a Moravian, but it was their influence that led him from seeing Christianity as "holy living" to seeing his walk with Jesus as an inner peace, a quiet confidence, a personal sense of experiencing Jesus as his own Savior and Lord. During his twenty months in Savannah, he met regularly with the Moravians, seeking their counsel. Every new Christian needs a "sponsor" just as much as a sober alcoholic in A.A. needs one.

In William Paul Young's best-selling novel *The Shack,* God says to the argumentative Mack:

"When you don't hear me the first time, I am not frustrated. That first time will be a building block to construct a bridge of healing that one day you will walk across." [73]

In 1926, Gilbert Rowe of Duke Divinity School wrote:

"Methodism learned and proclaimed the great truth that God deals directly with every [person] and is ready to impart to each one the best of all news – namely, that our sins are forgiven and each of us is a child of God." [74]

Wesley usually coupled the words "faith and practice." He wrote in a personal letter to a Mrs. Woodhouse in 1766:

"The spark of faith which you have received is of more value than all the world. O cherish it with all your might! Continually stir up the gift that is in you, not only continuing to hear God's Word preached, but by reading, by meditation, and above all by private prayer."

Wesley constantly had to resist charges from Anglican clergy that Methodists were excessive in the emotions that sometimes accompanied their release from guilt. Interestingly, he called his own experience on May 24, 1738, "an inward impression on the soul whereby the Spirit of God directly witnessed to my spirit that I am a child of God." He wrote in his diary, "I felt my heart strangely warmed." We need to note the word "strangely" in his testimony because Wesley was not a man given to emotionalism. With the word "strangely," he pointedly defined the witness of the Spirit as "an inner conviction" rather than a shallow frenzy.

Wesley did not make his Aldersgate experience the subject of future sermons or insist that everyone should have a similar experience. Some do, some don't. The norm that he advocated for conversion is what he called "transformation of the heart" so that conversion means to have a sense of being forgiven,

---

73 Op. Cit Young, 191.

74 Op. Cit, Rowe, 152.

being "clean," being loved. As a gospel hymn puts it, "He loved me 'ere I knew him and all my love is due him...."

Wesley repeatedly condensed all Methodist beliefs to "love God and love neighbor." What is so amazing about grace is that we "grow in grace." As the issues of life come and go, grace enables and empowers us to resist temptations and to overcome our addiction to various forms of sin. He used the terms of the clinic more than the terms of the court; therefore, to him salvation is our spiritual healing and renewed victory. Wesley often used the words, "trust and confidence" which are more immune to momentary feelings or specific doctrines. (We shall address these dimensions of grace in subsequent chapters.)

Looking unto Jesus, the Pioneer and Perfecter of our Faith

Almost all Christians will agree that only in Jesus do we see the perfectly revealed portrait of God. Jesus said, "Anyone who has seen me has seen the Father." (John 14:9b {NIV}) Then, though, we must ask, "What kind of God did he reveal?" God is "Holy Will," but God is more than that! God is also "Holy Love."

Holy Love can never be dormant; it must be expressed. It is never static, but dynamic. Love means something different in different relationships and in different life circumstances. "For the law was given through Moses; grace and truth came through Jesus Christ." (John 1:17 {NIV}) John's Gospel prologue affirms incarnation language that is very different from the nativity story we read in Matthew and Luke, but its message is irrefutable: "And the Word became flesh and made his dwelling among us...full of grace and truth." (John 1:14 {NIV}) "From the fullness of his grace, we have all received grace upon grace" (John 1:16 {NIV}).

In the book he co-authored with Paul Viola, Leonard Sweet wrote in 2010:

"According to Scripture, Jesus Christ (and not a doctrine about Him) is the truth. Jesus Christ (and not an ethic derived from his teaching) is the Way. In other words, both "God's TRUTH and God's WAY are embodied in a living, breathing person – Jesus Christ." [75]

We are called to a relationship with God who in Jesus Christ showed Himself to be a God of redeeming love. The mission on which God sent the Bethlehem baby, whose birth the angel announced as "good news of great joy which shall be to all people," is the same as the Savior of all humankind who died on the cross. Jesus inseparably unites incarnation and the atonement.

If we are to understand the essence of Christianity, we must see both the manger and the cross in the context of God's expression of love recorded in John 3:16. God loved fallen humanity so much that God sent Jesus on a rescue mission! Len Sweet is so right: "God's Truth and God's Way are embodied in God's Son who gives us 'life more abundantly.'"

Jesus was more than a moral influence. Jesus' death on the cross was not to pay a ransom to the devil in exchange for our redemption. Nor should we interpret God's reconciling love in Jesus in the Old Testament paradigm of a sacrificial lamb being slain as a substitute for the sins of the people. Rather we should see Jesus' death as God's revelation of his "love that will not let us go." We affirm this every time we repeat one of the Bible's most well-known verses: "God so loved the world that he gave (at His initiative) His only Son, that whoever (responds affirmatively) with belief in Him shall not perish but have eternal life."

Albert Outler said at the 1974 Fondren lectures at SMU: "Even overwhelmed by our human lot with all our sin and life's tragedies, Jesus revealed God's love and, on the cross, demonstrated God's love, giving us hope beyond any human horizon–hope in, through, and beyond tragedy. The Christian gospel is not that Jesus appeased God's wrath on the cross, but that he was and is the agent of the Father's redemptive compassion." [76]

---

75 Sweet, Leonard; *Viola, Paul, Jesus Manifesto,* Thomas Nelson, 2010, 80.

76 Op. Cit., Outler, *Theology in the Wesleyan Spirit,* 63.

Jesus said, "I have called you my friends for everything that I learned from my Father I have made known to you." (John 15:15 {NIV}) He said to his disciple, Philip, "Anyone who has seen me has seen the Father." (John 14:9 {NIV})

Charles Wesley spoke for many of us when we feel "down on ourselves" or "in a funk":

"Amazing love, how can it be that thou, my God, shouldst die for me?"

Ted Campbell aptly notes, "Our emphasis on God's love does not contradict our belief in God's power, but Methodist devotion stresses divine love." He also says, "The Christian's pilgrimage, from start to finish, is undergirded by divine grace." [77]

In a letter replying to an unnamed correspondent, Wesley wrote on December 20, 1751:

"God loves you; therefore obey him. Christ died for you; therefore die to sin. Christ is risen; therefore rise in the image of God. Christ liveth forevermore; therefore, live to God till you live with him in glory." [78]

Wesley continued in his letter, "So we preached; and so you believed. This is the scriptural way, the Methodist way, the true way. God grant that we may never turn there from, to the right hand or to the left."

It is here and in similar personal letters as well as sermons that we discover and define the core "fundamental" of our belief: God is love.

In Charles Wesley's epic poem/hymn, *O Come Thou Traveler Unknown*, we find this Christian fundamental expressed so poignantly:

"Who I ask thee, who art thou? Tell me thy name and tell me now.

---

77 Op. Cit. Campbell, 46.

78 Op. Cit., Outler, JWW Vol. 24, 224.

Wrestling I will not let thee go till thy name, thy nature know.

Speak, or thou never hence shall move, and tell me if thy name is love.

'Tis Love! 'tis Love! Thou diedst for me, I hear thy whisper in my heart,

The morning breaks, the shadows flee, pure Universal Love Thou art;

To me, to all, thy mercies move – Thy nature and thy name is Love." [79]

Wesley insisted that the capstone of being created in the image of God is being endowed by God with human liberty. When God's love is so thoroughgoing that it sets the loved one free, God willfully diminishes his power. The freedom God gives us by his grace can be distorted by our resistance, hypocrisy, or just sheer independence. We can throw God's love back in his face, and say with Frank Sinatra, "I'll do it my way." So love, even God's love, is a risk; love is vulnerable. In any relationship, divine or human, when love is rejected, the initiator of love must make a decision –to continue loving or to withdraw love. Even in the Old Testament, we repeatedly hear the words describing God's love as "steadfast love." He never gave up on Israel.

Human love often depends on reciprocity: "I will love you if" or "I will love you so long as…" (and we add a condition.) God's love is steadfast, immovable, and never-ending. John Greenleaf Whittier, a Quaker, has us sing this:

"I know not where His islands lift their fronded palms in air; I only know I cannot drift beyond God's love and care."

The love of God is portrayed poignantly in Jesus' parable that we call "The Prodigal Son." German theologian Helmut Thielicke correctly insisted it should be called "The Parable of

---

79 *The United Methodist Hymnal*, United Methodist Publishing House, 1989, Hymn #387.

the Waiting Father." In 1642, when Rembrandt was an old man, he painted his famous *"Return of the Prodigal Son,"* an amazing revelation of the parable's deeper meaning. The central figure is not the son who has returned home, nor the sulking elder brother in the shadow. Rather it is the father, still wealthy as the red robe depicts, but now old and blind. The left hand is the strong clasping hand of a male; the right hand is the caressing hand of a woman! These were the hands that in love never let the boy go.

Rembrandt's painting gives no resemblance of a courtroom where justice is to be administered, or a mediator's desk where a deal is to be struck. The picture portrays nothing of a paternal lecture about bad behavior, immoral relationships, or squandered inheritance – or a demand that the son be willing to "obey the rules of the house" if he is re-admitted. Rather, there is an overwhelmingly warm and loving welcome.

As one studies the picture, the Scripture seems to appear before one's eyes: "My son who was lost is found. Put shoes on his feet and rings on his fingers and a robe on his shoulder. Kill the fatted calf." (Luke 15: 22-24 {NIV}) The same chapter of Luke that records the parable of "The Waiting Father" tells us, "...there will be more rejoicing in heaven over one sinner who repents than over ninety-nine righteous persons who do not need to repent." (Luke 15:7 {NIV})

Henri Nouwen, Dutch priest and famous author, sat in St. Petersburg for five hours, searching for every clue in the Rembrandt. Then he wrote a book, *Return of the Prodigal Son.* Nouwen tells how his study of this picture changed his ministry and his life. The message seared itself on Nouwen's soul – God is love.

Few preachers or writers can contemporize Scripture more pointedly than Leonard Sweet. In the book he co-authored with Frank Viola, *A Jesus Manifesto,* Sweet writes about Jesus' miracle at the wedding feast in Cana of Galilee:

"Watch him at a wedding in Cana. According to the custom

of that day, the bridegroom was responsible for the food and wine. You know the story; the wine ran out. It represented a social disgrace – a grave oversight on the part of the bridegroom. Jesus created a finer wine than the wine that had run out. In one brilliant stroke of compassion, Jesus Christ removes the bridegroom's shame. He supplies the lack. He covers the mistake. He removes the disgrace. He reverses the failure. He makes the bridegroom a champion! What a Christ!" [80]

We see Jesus acting out the love of God in his conversation with the Samaritan woman at Jacob's Well. Our familiarity with the story can cause us to miss the depth of love that it unpacks. The woman has been battered, abused, shamed and forgotten. (John 4:1-42 {NIV}) To the Jews, she was a Samaritan of ill repute – a five-time divorcée and current live-in. Our Lord breaks all social conventions by talking to her in public, but that's not all. He shares with her one of the greatest truths that a human being can know: "Believe me, woman, the time is coming when you will worship the Father neither on this mountain nor in Jerusalem....The time is coming and now is when true worshipers shall worship the Father in Spirit and in Truth." He then stayed two days in a Samaritan village, and, presumably 1) stayed in their houses, 2) ate with them, and 3) used their utensils. Almost every line in this narrative breaks the custom of the Pharisees. This is another revelation of the depth and breadth of God's love.

Now turn in your Bible to another familiar and strange encounter that Jesus had. We read it in John 8:1-11. The religious leaders brought to Jesus a woman caught in "the very act of committing adultery." Their law of Moses commanded that she be stoned. What would Jesus do? Each had a stone ready to begin the horrible death. He knelt and began scribbling in the sand, stood up, and asked, "Let anyone among you who is with-

---

80 Op. Cit. Sweet, 164.

out sin be the first to throw a stone at her." One by one, they let their stones drop from their hands and slinked away. It was a powerful demonstration of how Jesus reflected God's love for sinners.

A contemporary Christian song ends with the essential message of the Christian Gospel:

"I hear you whispering my name.

You (God) say, 'My love for you will never change.

My love for you will never change.'"

In the Old Testament, the message of the entire book of Hosea is to convey God's never-ending love. The young prophet is asked to use his own life as a parable of God's love for Israel. Hosea married a prostitute. They had three children. Then, Gomer left Hosea and went back to the "red light district" from which she had come. Years passed until one day at the local slave market, Hosea recognized as his wife, the pathetic old woman on whom no one would bid. Hosea bought her back and took her home. So it is that God never gives up on us even if we waste years of our life and say, "No" to God's love.

Far too many of God's children have lost their way in life. For some, that lostness has led to behavior they cannot change, substances they cannot kick, relationships they cannot break, habits they cannot overcome, and guilt they cannot shake. Some have become disenchanted with the Church and cannot "shake it." For some, life has simply lost its meaning. Even the best of psychological counseling cannot do what a manifestation of the love of God can do. When we have lost our way, we cannot get home alone. Fanny Crosby's gospel hymn had us singing accurately:

"Jesus is tenderly calling thee home...

Jesus is calling the weary to rest;

Bring him thy burden and thou shalt be blest...."

76

We Wesleyans insist that Jesus did not die to placate the anger of God but rather to show us how much God loves us. As William Paul Young writes in *The Shack*:

"What you see as chaos, I see as fractal. All things must unfold, even though it puts all those I love in a world of horrible tragedies – even the one closest to me." [81]

Young's fictional character, "Mack," responds, "You are talking about Jesus, aren't you? What did he accomplish by dying?"

God answers regarding Jesus' mission: "The substance of everything that love purposed from before the foundation of Creation. Reconciliation is a two-way street and I have done my part. It is not the nature of love to force a relationship but it is the nature of love to open the way." [82]

From these diverse sources, we find testimony to Wesley's position that God's major attribute is love!

---

81 Op. Cit., Young 191.

82 Ibid. 192.

Questions for Discussion and Reflection

Believing that God loves us "warts and all" is not easy! Was this chapter helpful in taking a new step in your own faith journey?

Which quote from the Bible or other books was most helpful?

Do you feel "spiritually inferior" if you cannot name the time and place when you were saved? Does the "journey" paradigm help?

Where did you find yourself in disagreement with the author?

"If we take this in its utmost extent it will include all that is wrought in the soul by what is frequently termed 'natural conscience,' but more properly, 'preventing grace'; all the 'drawing' of the Father, the desires after God, which, if we yield to them, increase more and more; all that 'light' wherewith the Son of God 'enlighteneth everyone that cometh into the world,' showing every man 'to do justly, to love mercy, and to walk humbly with his God.'"

From Sermon "Scriptural Way of Salvation"

Notice the language in the following quote. It is more like a clinic than a court!

"You are in the hands of a wise Physician, who is lancing your sores in order to heal them. He has given you now the spirit of fear, but it is in order to reveal the spirit of love and of a sound mind. You have now received the spirit of bondage; is it not the forerunner of the spirit of adoption? He is not afar off! Look up! And expect him to cry in your heart, 'Abba (Father).' He is nigh that justifieth."

A Wesley letter to a seeker

Here Wesley is quoting a Quaker mystic:

"'My son, give me thy heart' is the language of the great God to every rational creature. 'Give me thy heart for it was I who made it, it was I that gave it to thee! It was I that bestowed its vital motion, and that for no other end but to direct and incline it toward me/ I am thy true good; in me alone canst thou find rest for thy soul; all the springs of thy happiness are in me. Therefore...give me thy heart. 'Tis I alone who can reward thy love.'"

Wesley's quote of John Norris (1657-1711)

Chapter Five

Preparing Grace:
God's Undergirding and Nudging Us

"There will be more rejoicing in heaven over one sinner who repents than over ninety-nine righteous persons who do not need to repent."

Luke 15:10

We noted earlier that the best Wesleyan scholars, including Ted Runyan, Richard Heitzenrater, and Randy Maddox have documented that Wesley's "grace theology" should be described with the Latin words *"via salutis"* (way of salvation) rather than *"ordo salutis"* (order of salvation). Calvinists scholars like "order," but that takes salvation away from a relationship and places it in a series of "states" or "stages" riveted together like links in a chain. According to Maddox, such a paradigm makes the Christian life more a standard set of abrupt transitions in status rather than a developing relationship between us and God as our Father. *"Via salutis,"* on the other hand, sees our relationship with our Lord as a continuing journey as we experience more of what Wesley called "grace upon grace." [83] God's grace "prevenes" or precedes our responsive faith.

Steve Harper is "right on" in writing:

"Grace is grace. You do not have one kind of grace for one life season and another kind for some other situation. We simply define grace in differing ways because of how we

---

83 Op. Cit. Maddox, *Responsible Grace*, 157-158.

experience it. Grace comes to us as little children and as octogenarians on our death beds. It accomplishes different effects and evokes different responses, but it is all grace." [84]

God's love is a seeking, pro-active love. In Genesis 1:27, we see that God created us in God's own image, in perfectly harmonious relationship. Then, with sad suddenness, in Genesis 3, we read of Adam and Eve's disobedience resulting in the "fall" and subsequent estrangement, alienation, and brokenness of this Creator-creature relationship. However, as real and deep and destructive as sin is, our sin does not define us. Our creation as a son or daughter of the most High God defines us and that is indelible!

Thomas Oden was a professor at Drew Theological Seminary and a superlative student of Wesley. In his two-volume book, John Wesley's Teachings, he draws heavily on Wesley's sermon, "On Working Out Our Own Salvation" the text for which was Philippians 2:12-13. He gives us a superb etymology for a word Wesley loved and we never heard of: "Prevenient Grace." "Prevenient" is a word whose meaning has changed radically since its Latin root! Today "prevent" means to obstruct, hinder, or stop." In Latin *nos praeveniente* meant "the grace that comes before." But before what? The answer should be explained with every infant baptism which is a splendid illustration of prevenient grace because "it comes before any conscious personal experience of God. Wesley was saying that the first move is God's, not ours." [85] That is true for the child who is not baptized or who is!

Since Wesley believed that our being made in the image of God is indelible – a state that he called "original righteousness" – he was often accused of not believing in original sin. Not so! In his sermon, "Original Sin," Wesley clearly preached and wrote, "All men are by nature not only sick, but dead in trespasses and sins." But then Wesley asked, "What is the religion of Jesus Christ? Is it God's method of healing a soul which is

---

84 Op. Cit., Harper, 40.

85 Ibid., 40.

thus diseased? The great Physician of Souls applies medicine to heal this sickness; to restore human nature that is totally corrupted in all its faculties." [86] The song is right, "There is a balm in Gilead to make the wounded whole; there is a balm in Gilead to heal the sinsick soul." God's will is for us to get spiritually well.

When John Wesley agreed to the Methodists in America's forming an official denomination in 1784, he sent an abridged version of the *Thirty-nine Articles of Religion of the Anglican Church for the new American Methodists.* Wesley kept unchanged the article entitled "Of Free Will":

"The condition of man after the fall of Adam is such that he cannot turn and prepare himself, by his own natural strength and works, to faith or calling upon God; wherefore we have no power to do good works, pleasant and acceptable to God, without the grace of God by Christ's prevening us {preparing us, assisting us} that we may have a good will, and working within us when we have that good will." [87]

As Lovett Weems teaches us, "God comes to us first. Before we ever take a step, God is there. Within every life, from the beginning, is this simple, basic, elemental, initiating presence of God." [88]

The Bible is filled with examples of God's "speaking" to judges, prophets, priests, kings, and "ordinary" women and men.

So in God's prevenient grace, God is "nudging" or whispering to our inmost soul. Arminius and Wesley, as Albert Outler euphemistically put it, believed in "total depravity, but not tee-total depravity." Thomas Oden wrote that "persons still have a degree of liberty to be self-governing, otherwise we

---

86 Op. Cit., Wesley, John, Sermon, "Original Sin," JWW, Vol. 2, 184.

87 *UMC Book of Discipline Article of Religion VIII.*

88 Weems, Lovett, *John Wesley's Message Today,* Abingdon, 1982, Discipleship Resources, 23.

would be robots under the total control of God or Satan or the determinism of behavioral psychology." [89] Methodists believe that, with all limitations of any sort, God still works within our "fallen" human nature to draw us back to the relationship with Him that we see described ever so briefly in Genesis 1:27.

> "God's image is not totally eradicated by original sin. What Calvin called "common grace," Wesley preached as, "This faculty is what is usually meant by "natural conscience." Though in one sense it may be natural because it is found in all men; yet properly speaking, conscience is not natural, but a supernatural gift of God, above all his natural endowments. It is not from nature, but from the Son of God, that God gives 'the true light which enlighteneth every man that cometh into the world.'" [90] (John 1:4, 9 {NIV})

Salvation begins with God's loving, seeking initiative, even while we are still "dead in sin." In his sermon "The Image of God" Wesley preached from Colossians 3:10, "Yet our merciful, though rejected, Creator would not forsake even the depraved work of his own hands, but provided for him, and offered to him a means of being renewed after the image of him that created him." [91] Wesley is insisting that in spite of the universality of original sin, that the image of God in which we were created is not totally obliterated because of prevenient grace.

Instead of the archaic Latin words, "prevenient grace," let's call the preliminary working of the Holy Spirit "God's preparatory grace." [92] Wesley called it a "deep thing of God," "the inward impression on the soul." Oden points out, "Preparatory grace is the lowest gear in the drive train of grace that enables one to move from inertia (as in infancy). We have no way of raising ourselves to new life. Preparatory grace makes this miracle

---

89 Oden, Thomas, *John Wesley's Teachings,* Vol. 2, Zondervan, 1994, 138.

90 Op. Cit, Wesley, John, Sermon, *"On Conscience,"* Outler, Ed. Vol. 3, 482.

91 Ibid. Wesley, John, Sermon, *"The Image of God,"* Vol. 4, 293.

92 Op. Cit., Oden, Vol. 2, 137.

happen! The will may be drawn toward saving grace." [93] Many
of us remember from childhood the story of young Samuel's
hearing God's calling him in the middle of the night. (I Samuel
3:1-21 {NIV}) Regardless of our childhood, youth, adulthood, or
psychological disposition, God occasionally "speaks" to us in
our conscience, during a sermon, while driving, when reading
the Bible, or in ICU! Sadly, there is one catch; grace, like human
love, can be resisted or embraced. This is a major difference
between Arminius' and Wesley's doctrine and Augustine's and
Calvin's. They believe that for God's Elect, grace is irresistible;
we believe that every person is "elected to be saved," but that
any can resist grace.

In Charles Wesley's account of his own journey, he says,
"I heard thee whisper in my heart." God's grace is manifest to
us before we have a consciousness of God's love for us, or any
desire to follow Jesus. Wesley did not minimize the pervasiveness of original sin, but as Wesley Theological Seminary professor Lovett Weems writes, "Sin is not what God wants for us.
God is not content for us to experience nothing but the seduc-
tive pull of original sin; so God, even in our sinfulness, comes
to us in grace." [94] As we sing our faith, we say that God comes
to us in a "love that will not let me go; I rest my weary soul in
thee." [95]

We cannot save ourselves. Paul says, "No one can say 'Jesus
is Lord' except by the Holy Spirit" (I Corinthians 12:3 {NIV}), but
the good news is that the Holy Spirit works in the conscience of
every person. (Romans 1:20 {NIV})

Prevenient grace is entirely the work of God. Author Steve
Harper points out, "Prevenient grace is to some a novel idea, but
it is crucial in understanding Wesley's order of salvation." Wesley
called it the awakening of the soul. This is grace 'whispering to
our heart,' awakening our deadened natural conscience, which
Wesley believed 'makes us more or less uneasy when we act

93 Ibid., 138.

94 Op. Cit., Weems,22.

95 Matheson, George, 1982, Hymn: *"O Love That Will Not Let Me Go,"* 1982.

contrary to the light of our own conscience.' [96]

I had the privilege of sitting in Bristol, England, under the teaching of British Methodist Rupert Davies, an expert in the mind and soul of Wesley. I heard him say what later appeared in his book, *Methodism:* "The relentless teaching about sin is alleviated by the consideration that fallen man still has the law of God written on his heart and a conscience with which to discern it." [97] Davies then enumerated three prevenient gifts that he believes are provided to fallen humanity:

- **the moral "inner light" of conscience**
- **the capacity for reason**
- **the freedom to hear and receive the Word of God**

All of these played a pivotal role in the development of Wesleyan theology, and all lead us to very different conclusions about God's grace than does Calvinism. They refer to the image of God as recorded in Genesis 1:27!

What Was Wesley's Interpretation of John 14:6?

As we discuss prevenient or preparational grace, we must ask, "What did Wesley say about the people of other cultures who never hear about Jesus?" Does John 14:6 mean that they are lost, as some rigid Fundamentalists have said? Wesley says, "No." Let us remember that contrary to many whose education and doctrinal influence is very provincial and parochial, Wesley had access to the greatest libraries in the world at Oxford University and on the British Empire, "the sun never set." He was a voracious reader and acquainted himself with all the primary text of other religions. Wesley had read the *Qur'an* in its entirety – something very few Christians can claim even today! He read some in the *Vedas of Hinduism* and had at least a precursory knowledge of Buddhism. He knew the wisdom sayings of Confucius.

---

96 Op. Cit., Harper. 39.

97 Davies, Rupert, *Methodism,* Epworth Press, 1985, 85.

In response to those who think non-Christians are lost, Wesley had a cosmopolitan cultural exposure like Augustine who was a member of the Roman Empire in the fourth and fifth centuries. In his sermon, "On Conscience," Wesley quoted Francis Hutcheson, professor of philosophy at Glasgow University:

"Every man has a moral sense whereby he approves of benevolence and disapproves of cruelty. We are pained at the misery of a fellow creature and pleased at his deliverance from it. Yea, he is uneasy when he himself has done a cruel action and pleased when he has done a generous one." [98]

Tom Oden, in reflecting on this dimension of prevenient grace that enlightens the intellect and conscience of every person, noted that Wesley kept in mind these observations:

- Unregenerate people have reliable knowledge and act in ways commonly called "good."
- Even under the conditions of paganism, cultures have developed a comparatively orderly life.
- Natural man possesses the capacity to distinguish between good and evil through conscience.
- *The disciplines of science, art, architecture, mathematics, astronomy, horticulture, and animal husbandry have advanced in pagan civilizations.*[99]

In Wesley's sermon, "Working Out Our Own Salvation," published in Arminian magazine in 1785, he opened with these words:

"Some great truths, as the being and attributes of God, and the difference between moral good and evil, were known in some measure to the heathen world; the traces of them are to be found in all nations; so that in some sense

---

98 Op. Cit., Wesley, Sermon, *"On Conscience,"* JWW Vol. 3, 483-484.

99 Op. Cit., Oden, Vol. 2, 150.

it may be said to every child of man, 'He hath showed thee, O man, what is good; even to do justly, to love mercy, and to walk humbly with thy God.' (Micah 6:8 {NIV}) *With this truth God has, in some measure, 'enlightened everyone that cometh into the world.' (John 1:9 {NIV}) And thereby, those who have not the law (of Moses) 'are a law unto themselves.' (Romans 2:14 {NIV}) They show that the substance of the law, though not the letter, is 'written in their hearts' (Jeremiah 31:33 {NIV}) by the same hand which wrote the commandments on the tablets of stone (for Moses); their conscience also bearing them witness whether they act suitably thereafter or not."* [100]

In this same sermon, Wesley continued,

"No man living is entirely destitute of what is vulgarly called "natural conscience." But this is not natural; it is more properly termed 'preventing grace.' Every man has a great or less measure of this which waiteth not for the call of man. Everyone has sooner or later good desires, although the generality of men stifle them before they produce much fruit. Everyone has some glimmering ray of light which sooner or later, more or less, enlightens everyone who comes into the world. So no one sins because he has not grace, but because he does not use the grace which he hath." [101]

All these Wesley references clearly state that Wesley believed that an important dimension of prevenient grace is the grace that is common to all humankind. Wesley had found this in Georgia with his work among the Native Americans and his work in South Carolina with Africans, and in his study of other religions. Colin Williams of Australian Methodism is our teacher here: "Wesley believed that those who do not hear the gospel are judged according to their response to this prevenient

---

100 Ibid. Vol 3, 199-200.

101 Ibid. 207.

grace by which Christ works within them in a hidden way." [102] They are like the patriarchs and prophets. This is the inference of Paul in Romans 1:20.

In John 14:6, Jesus is saying literally, "No one comes to the Father but through me." Other religions did not and do not have that concept of God. Only Jesus revealed God as our Father, but people who follow their conscience are not lost.

Preparing Grace: "God's Whispers to the Soul"

The United Methodist Book of Discipline includes prevenient grace in its lists of "distinctive Wesleyan emphases":

"This grace prompts our first wish to please God, our first glimmer of understanding concerning God's will, and our 'first transient conviction' of having sinned against God." [103]

We see this manifest especially, but not exclusively, in children of Christian parents. Every parent should be certain that their children know well the story of God's speaking to Samuel as a boy. Long before I was mature enough to make a mature commitment to Jesus Christ as my Savior, my "conscience was my guide." This seeking love or prevenient grace is clearly an activity of God that nudges us toward repentance and being saved by our faith in God's grace. Learning Bible stories, being taught that Jesus loves us, going to church, serving as an acolyte, taking communion, and being loved by a supportive faith community are all "nudges" toward saving grace.

Can we resist these nudges? Absolutely. We can, in the words of an older Methodist generation "quench the Spirit." Still, the more conscience is shaped by Christian influences, the more likely that we will eventually respond positively.

In Disney's *Lion King*, Mufasa, the king of the lions, is killed, and his son, Simba, is cheated out of his inheritance.

---

102 Williams, Colin, *John Wesley's Theology Today*, Abingdon, 1989, 45.

103 *The Book of Discipline, The United Methodist Church*, United Methodist Publishing House, 2008, 46.

After Simba is betrayed by Scar and transported through the land of the evil hyenas to the culture of the meercats and warthogs, he is comfortable in his new identity. Finally, Rafiki rescues Simba and tells him that he is not a warthog. As the movie concludes, Rafiki takes Simba to a high rock with the jungle before them and says, "Simba, you are more than you have become." That is precisely what the Holy Spirit says to us in prevenient grace! While addicted to original sin, we have forgotten who we are – a child of the King!

Colin Williams again is our teacher. He writes, "Wesley is far from claiming that prevenient grace communicated through the Holy Spirit brings us into conformity with God's will or overcomes the residual effects of original sin." [104] If we respond affirmatively to God's "whispers to the soul," we are still a sinner as measured by absolute standards. What prevenient grace does, as we mature, is to bring us under conviction for our sin (a state) and our sins (the total package of our thoughts, words, and deeds). It meant a moment of soul truth.

Every person has a kairos moment, a "God moment" if you will, in which our past rolls by us like an old movie and we have some fear or guilt of what is going on with us. In the old days, this was called "coming under conviction." This is the work of the Holy Spirit. As William Abraham says it, "God has stepped into everyone's inner life to help us see what is wrong with us and to awaken us to a positive response." [105] Colin Williams has written, "Prevenient or preparing grace prepares us for the threshold of grace that God offers us. The man who obeys his quickened conscience 'comes to himself' and is ready to receive more grace – saving grace, redeeming grace, justifying grace!" [106]

Williams is most helpful as he continues to explicate the difference that prevenient grace brings to the theological contrast between Wesley and Calvin. Calvin was locked into

---

104 Op. Cit., Williams, 43.

105 Abraham, William, *Wesley for Armchair Theologians,* Westminster, 2005, 51.

106 Op. Cit. Williams, 43-44.

his logic of God's predestination. Wesley broke the chain of logic. Prevenient grace is God's "whisper to the heart" that we call conscience, the glimmer of residue from Genesis 1:27 {NIV} (original righteousness). The consequence is universal grace – free in all regardless of our disposition or doctrine, and free for all as Jesus promised: "Whoever comes to me I will never drive away." (John 6:37 {NIV}) Calvinists limit grace to the Elect. Sad.

In Wesley's sermon, "Witness of the Spirit I," he stressed the priority of the Spirit's prevenient and direct witness as the necessary precondition to forgiving grace or "blessed assurance of knowing one's sins forgiven." Again, the bottom line is that prevenient grace is divine initiative, witnessing to us that we need not remain in bondage to sin.

Logically, the sermon is based on Romans 8:16: "The Spirit himself testifies with our spirit that we are God's children." The implication is profoundly important. Regardless of our sin, our addictions, or the number of people we have hurt, God loves us and is proactively "whispering to our heart" that we are more than we have become.

There is so much good in what Rick Warren writes in *The Purpose of Christmas,* an example being:

"You were created as an object of God's love. He made you in order to love you. Every time your heart beats and every time you take a breath, God is saying, 'I love you.' He loves you when you don't feel his love as much as when you do. He loves you regardless of your performance, your moods, your actions, or your thoughts. His love for you is unchanging." [107]

He is so "point on" with this affirmation, but unfortunately, Warren immediately follows this beautiful insight with a brief return to his doctrine of predestination! It would be with his son's suicide that Warren could finally say on television, "God did not intend my son to die."

---

107 Oop. Cit.,Warren, *The Purpose of Christmas,* 2008, 22-23.

Other Dimensions of Prevenient Grace as Divine Initiative

There are two other dimensions of God's prevenient grace that come totally as a divine initiative:

One is what Jesus called "the Holy Comforter." When we are in our darkest hour and our faith is very weak–our hours of distress, fear, and grief– God is with us in ways we cannot understand. Someone has said, "When we reach the end of our rope, God has already tied a knot in it." When we are at our lowest ebb, we sense some higher power undergirding us and giving us the courage to "soldier on." We all have seen the poem, "Footprints in the Sand":

"'During the most trying periods of my life, there have been only one set of footprints.... 'Why, when I need you most, have you not been there for me?' The Lord replied, 'The times when you have seen only one set of footprints is when I was carrying you.'"

Paul assured us that God's grace is sufficient to carry us through our toughest times, our hardest hours, our worst circumstances. This, too, is prevenient grace.

Secondly, God never gives up on us. Ira Sankey, a Methodist and song leader for evangelist Dwight L. Moody in the late nineteenth century, became acquainted in Scotland with a local poem comparing God's seeking love with the Highlands shepherds' determination to never lose a sheep. One night Moody preached on Luke 15:1-7 and for the altar call turned to Sankey and said, "Sing something appropriate." That day in a local Scottish paper, Sankey had read a poem, "The Ninety and Nine." He went to the piano, hit an A-flat and began to sing from his soul the words of Elizabeth Clephane's poem to a tune never before rehearsed nor even created. It was a miraculous moment. Many came to Christ as their Savior that night in Scotland. Thousands have come to Christ with this poignant, moving narrative of God's highly personal, never-ending, seeking love (i.e. prevenient grace):

"'Lord, Thou hast here Thy ninety and nine, are they not enough for Thee?'

But the Shepherd answered, 'This of Mine has wandered away from Me,

And although the road be rough and steep, I go to the desert to find my sheep.'

Then through the mountains, thunder-riv'n, and up from the rocky steep,

There arose a glad cry to the gate of heav'n, 'Rejoice I have found my sheep!'

And the angels echoed around the throne, 'Rejoice for the Lord brings back his own!'" [108]

Francis Thompson, a Roman Catholic in London's Victorian Age, was a destitute opium addict for years. He was rescued by a Christian who reached out to him. Thompson's poem *"Hound of Heaven"* is so poignantly descriptive of God's love (i.e. prevenient grace):

"I fled him down the nights and down the days, I fled him down the arches of the years

I fled him down the labyrinthine ways of my own mind,

And in the mist of tears I hid from Him and under running laughter.

Up vista-ed slopes, I sped; And shot precipitated....

But with unhurrying chase and unperturbed pace, deliberate speed, majestic instancy

They beat – and a Voice beats more instant than the feet."

[God's response:]

"Oh that thou might'est seek in My arms, All, my child you fancy as lost!

---

108 Clephane, Elizabeth Cecilia (1830-1869).

Ah, fondest, blindest, weakest, I am He whom thou seekest!
Rise, clasp my hand and come!" [109]

Fanny Crosby, a devout Methodist, was blind from childhood. She wrote over 8,000 hymns. *"Rescue the Perishing,"* written in 1869, is about God's prevenient grace:

"Tho they are slighting Him still He is waiting, waiting the penitent child to receive;

Plead with them earnestly, plead with them gently; He will forgive if they only believe.

Down in the human heart, crushed by the Tempter, feelings lie buried that grace can restore

Touched by a loving heart, wakened by kindness, chords that were broken can vibrate once more."

Whether a child who was nurtured in the faith or a child who had no spiritual nurture, or an adult who had "sowed wild oats," or a person for whom faith has simply never come alive, God has made his move; now you can respond! Perkins School of Theology Professor William Abraham puts it so accurately in "everyday language": "Prevenient grace is the initial help God gives to everyone to see how grim things are and to form the first intention to get help." [110]

---

109 Thompson, Francis, The Hound of Heaven, Morehouse Publishing, 4, 7, 26.

110 Op. Cit., Abraham, 53.

Questions for Discussion and Reflection

Is the term "prevenient grace" new to you? Does it help to substitute "preparing" for Wesley's word "pre-venient"?

At some "God moment" in your life, have you felt convicted of your sinfulness? At some "God moment," have you felt God's "whispering to your heart?" Would you describe your forgiveness from God as "washed whiter than snow" from your sin? Do you have homework with God needing to be finished? If so, are you ready to finish it? Your reward is "peace that passes understanding."

Turn in your Bible to Revelation 3:20 and get a Holman Hunt picture off the internet of Christ at the Door. Have you unlatched the door from the inside? This is your role in salvation.

Remember the line I mentioned from *The Lion King*. Put in your name where Simba's is and listen to "Rafiki": "_____, you are more than you have become." Are you ready to "let go and let God get you in touch with the immortal diamond in your soul?"

Have you ever heard Ira Sankey's "Ninety and Nine" sung? Pull it up online. Can you identify with this portrayal of Luke 15:3-7: God's seeking you like the one sheep who strayed?

Did you find Francis Thompson's poem, "Hound of Heaven" comforting or disturbing? The bottom line is like Psalm 139:7-12. Again, pull up this poem online.

"He {God} made man in his own image, a spirit endued with understanding and liberty. Man, abusing that liberty, produced evil and brought sin and pain into the world. God permitted this in order to {give us} a fuller manifestation of his wisdom, justice, and mercy by bestowing on all who would receive it an infinitely greater happiness...."

John Wesley, 1782

In Albert Outler's words, "Wesley's sermon, 'Original Sin,' was in the logic of his soteriology, a major doctrinal statement in which he sought to compound the Latin tradition of total depravity with the Eastern Orthodox view of sin as disease, and is a sufficient answer to all simple-minded references to Wesley as a Pelagian."

Outler, Albert, *The Works of John Wesley*, V 2, Abingdon 1985, 171

"If we confess our sins, he who is faithful and just will forgive us our sins and purify us from all unrighteousness."

I John 1:9

"In his great mercy he has given us new birth into a living hope.... Though you have not seen him, you love him...you believe in him and are filled with an inexpressible and glorious joy, for you are receiving the goal of your faith, the salvation of your souls."

I Peter 1:3b, 8-9

"Salvation is the fundamental doctrine of the church."

John Wesley

Read Romans 10: 9-13.

Chapter Six

Being Saved Differently
We are not "Cookie-cutter" Christians

"Since we are utterly incapable of living the glorious lives that God wills, God did it for us! Out of sheer grace he put us in right standing with himself. A pure gift. He got us out of the mess we're in and restored us to where he always wanted us to be. And he did it by means of Jesus Christ. Having faith in him sets us clear."

Romans 3:21-26 {The Message}

In our lives, through natural conscience, invitational preaching, a campfire, a small group in a college dorm, walking in the woods, upon the loss of a grandparent or parent, or a conversation of what Wesley called "holy conversation," we can get "under conviction" of our sinfulness. Indeed, this can come on our death bed as it did to Voltaire, the famous eighteenth century French atheist. Whoever we are and whatever our journey, we Methodists believe that it is God's purpose that every person celebrates the inner peace of saving faith.

William Abraham puts it this way:

"At some point, the individual on the way to the Kingdom must see what is at stake and look to God for forgiveness; God alone can supply relief to the soul. Coming to faith is not so much making a decision as it is waiting for God." [111]

---

111 Ibid, Abraham, 67.

The Varieties of Experiencing God's Saving Grace

Grace is grace, but after years of God's preparing grace, we have a "God moment" that calls for a response. Whether in one's late childhood, teen years, or adult life, God's nudge is God's call for our response.

Randy Maddox calls this "Response-able grace." In this rather mystical moment, God seems so near. We sense the "still, small voice," the urge to repent, the "light" that comes on in our mind and heart. We have a free will choice: we can accept or resist. We make a decision, a decision rooted in our God-given human liberty – "Yes," "No," or "Later." Because we are free to make the choice of our preference, it is a moral choice.

That free will response is what Randy Maddox names "synergistic grace" in contrast to Calvin's doctrine of "monergistic" grace. Calvin insisted that only God is the agent in salvation. Maddox interprets Wesley's synergism as "grace-empowered human cooperation" with the nudging of the Holy Spirit.[112] He cites Wesley's sermon, "On Working Out Our Own Salvation:" "It is God that worketh in us both to will and to do.'" [113] This means that being saved from our sins is not just a matter of human will, but of human response to the nudging of the Holy Spirit–our faith in God's grace.

It is again Dr. Maddox who so helpfully interprets Wesley concerning the inherent saving grace of the sacraments. Whether taking communion, attending worship, or praying, all can be sheer ritual unless "one recognizes and responds to God's gracious prevenience expressed through them." [114]

Synergism is being "in sync" as when two clocks indicate the same time, two dancers keep in step with each other, or we say, "We are on the same page." So it is with God and us; we

---

112 Op. Cit, Maddox. 91.

113 Ibid. 92.

114 Ibid., 196.

can be "in sync" or "out of sync." If "in sync," we make a positive response to the prevenient nudging at our inmost soul. We are now near to the kingdom of God. We kneel on what Wesley called the "porch of repentance," sense the waiting Father's forgiveness, rise, and go through "the threshold of grace." Yes, it is what is colloquially called, "being saved."

Wesley had observed enough persons "coming home" to know that some come gradually and some come suddenly; some come quietly and some come with tears of joy. A more accurate description would be that having responded positively to God's prevenient nudging, we can say, "I have been saved, I am being saved, I will be saved."

Saving grace is the experience of grace that comes with our decision to follow Jesus, but we must avoid a "cookie-cutter" concept of saving grace. Christians are like snowflakes; no two of us are identical. That is why the question, "When were you saved?" has an easy answer for some, but not for others. We might be but a child saying "yes" to what we have learned in Sunday School or home about God's love for us, and being confirmed in our faith as a maturing youth.

Or, we might have journeyed toward home slowly as we are nurtured in church or in a Christian relationship. Or, we might be the "prodigal" who came to the end of one's rope, only to find that God tied a knot in the rope to which we can hang on! Or, we might have had a life changing "God moment" at a crisis time in life.

The one thing that all persons affirming to be a Christian have in common is the theme of Gloria Gaither's hymn written in 1963, *"He Touched Me":*

> *"...then the hand of Jesus touched me, and now I am no longer the same...*
>
> *something happened and now I know, he touched me and made me whole."*

We hear the same theme in Charles Wesley's hymn written in 1742:

"...the grace unspeakable I now receive; through faith I see thee face to face and live!

I have not wept or strived in vain – Thy nature and Thy name is Love."

Being saved is not a *fait accompli* nor is it static. It usually means a conscious acceptance of God's forgiveness for our sin and accepting Jesus as our Savior. Then begins the lifelong journey of giving thought, word, and deed to Jesus as the Lord of our life. So often this includes resisting temptations and having "victories in Jesus" until we draw our last breath. Wesley loved Philippians 2:5 (NIV) where we read Paul's words, "In your relationships with one another, have the same mindset as Christ Jesus" That requires some spiritual discipline and trust that God's grace is sufficient for us even in our life extremities.

For the Christian journey, temptations, rough patches, and unprecedented issues make the pilgrim's an uneven path. Paul wrote to the Philippians, "...for I have learned to be content whatever the circumstances. I know what it is to be in need, and I know what it is to have plenty. I have learned the secret of being content in any and every situation. I can do everything through Him who gives me strength." (Philippians 4:11-13 (NIV)) Also, along with human issues, the good news is that God is full of surprises! Wesley called it "grace upon grace."

Rather than always employing "quick fix" answers like "praying the sinner's prayer" or memorizing "Four Spiritual Laws," or "making a decision for Christ," we need to familiarize ourselves with the encounters Jesus had with such a diversity of persons in his own ministry. Nothing in the Gospels indicates that Jesus had a "prescription" to jot down for each of them and certainly did not give each the same invitation to discipleship. Think of The Twelve whom we often call his "disciples." What a variety of places people were in their own lives when Jesus said, "Follow me." Peter, James, and John were fishers, Matthew was a quisling tax collector, Simon was a terrorist, Judas Iscariot wanted a military victor to throw off the yoke of Rome, etc. etc.

Review in your Bible the diversity of people whom Jesus engaged – lepers, Roman army occupation officers, prostitutes, quislings, schizophrenics, Zaccheus the wealthy businessman with crooked ethics, the Samaritan woman at Jacob's well, the woman caught in the "very act of adultery" and Nicodemus, the Pharisee who was a member of the Sanhedrin.

Jesus said to the man who had lain on his mat in self-pity beside a pool for thirty-eight years, "Do you want to be made well? Stand up; take your mat and walk." Masochism is a psychological dysfunctionality. Repentance means "get up; get with it, and get over it." In Romans 5:5 {NIV} we read, "...hope does not disappoint us because God's love has been poured into our hearts through the Holy Spirit that has been given to us." Jesus did not have a "pat" invitation, but one that interfaced with the life situation, the personal disposition, and the faith journey of each. As we approach "What it means to be saved," we have to do our biblical homework rather than adopting a "one size fits all" statement.

We categorically do not believe that some are "elected," leaving others to be on the outside of grace. Charles Wesley taught this universal grace through a hymn:

"Come sinners to the gospel feast; let <u>every</u> soul be Jesus' guest

Ye need not one be left behind; for God hath bidden <u>all</u> mankind."

Here we differ from the Calvinists who insist that Jesus' atonement was limited to those whom God elects to save. We believe that Jesus died for everyone. Wesley considered the crowning dimension of being made in the image of God to be "human liberty." We are not marionettes on the end of a string, nor pre-programmed computer chips; we are free moral agents. We have the free will to make good choices and bad choices; both bear consequences.

Aldersgate was unique to John Wesley. Very few responsible scholars deny that he was a Christian prior to that experience. Wesley called his grace theology "experimental divinity." Faith is a disposition of the heart, made possible by the grace of God given to all who allow the Holy Spirit to awaken and grow, as Paul put it, "all who are led by the Spirit of God." (Romans 8:14-18 {NIV}) Saving grace came differently in Wesley's England, in Asbury's colonial America, and to us today. "Becoming a Christian" is admittedly "different strokes for different folks." We are ill-advised to negate another person's religious experience.

All journeys are different. Some of us accepted Jesus as children with little more emotion or analysis than the song, "Into my heart, into my heart, come into my heart, Lord Jesus." Such a conversion is like the bud opening as a blossom or a rising sun over the ocean. On the other hand, some people have repeatedly pushed God away. They virtually say to God what Governor Felix said to Paul, "You may leave. When I find it convenient, I will send for you." (Acts 24:25 {NIV})

Others describe their homecoming to God as a specific point in time as an instantaneous life changer–"O happy day that fixed my choice." I saw that in my father's conversion. He was not reared in church and did not go until he was forty-five years old. It was then that he heard the testimony of a man well known for making bootleg whiskey. He and Daddy had been elementary school classmates. He did not rise from the altar with any display of emotion, but we saw an immediate and lasting change in his lifestyle, beginning the next morning at breakfast. For the first time ever, he bowed his head and asked the blessing! Thereafter, he took us to church!

My journey was quite different from my father's. I came to Christ incrementally as I matured. I have certainly disappointed the good Lord and significant mentors in my life, but I never remember a time when I did not want to follow Jesus. I have been "churched" all my life. In a small rural church, I was building the wood fire in winter and mowing the pathetically thin grass in summer by the time I was ten years old.

Nevertheless, I do recall a special "God moment." When I was twelve I was chosen to have the prayer at a 4-H Camp vespers. I remember so well that those of us in the program walked around the head of the lake in candlelight procession singing. The words were God's "whispering to my heart." I remember the lyrics so well:

> *"To the knights in the days of old keeping watch on the mountain heights*
>
> *Came a vision of Holy Grail and a voice through the waiting night: 'Follow, follow the gleam.'*
>
> *And we who would serve the king and loyally him obey,*
>
> *In the consecrate silence know that the challenge still holds today*
>
> *'Follow, follow, follow the gleam of the Light that shall bring the dawn."*

I was deeply moved by that little procession and those words. Then I stepped onto a large granite boulder, looked over the darkened lake waters to two hundred campers with candles, and led a prayer. It was less than a month before my twelfth birthday. I had never heard "Follow the Gleam" sung before nor have I heard these words in Crusader idiom sung since. I went to my cabin. God's preparing grace had been guiding me since my birth. Now came the time for my response by repenting of my sins and accepting Jesus as my personal savior. I had no vision; I did not even leave my bunk to kneel in prayer. I only remember simply saying in my mind, "Yes, I want to be a Christian." What those words meant to a twelve-year-old farm kid was very different than what they meant as I became older, but the die was cast. That was June, 1947; my daddy died in September.

Wesley's Metaphor of "yard, porch, and house" of Working Out Our Salvation

The "Methodist way" of seeing scriptural salvation can be seen through the life journey of John Wesley reflected in his sermons, journals, diaries, and letters. To be faithful to the premise of this book, we must review Wesley's own understanding of *via salutis* or "way of salvation." Therefore, we hope the following can be a means of bringing persons to faith in Christ.

I find as helpful Wesley's paradigm of a house with a yard and a porch as a way of picturing our coming to Jesus. Let's expand that image to an image of the grounds or hedges surrounding the house to represent what we have called "preparing grace." Whether someone is a child with Christian parents, a "wild oats" youth, a substance abuse victim, a "successful" person who realizes there is more to life than materialism, or a person from another religious culture, Wesley's metaphor is a helpful explanation of coming to faith.

Wesley preached for an "awakening of the soul." Once we hear the Savior calling, "Follow, follow me," our soul is awakened, and we are "under conviction" and convinced of our need for outside help. We can say, "yes." We, like the "prodigal son" in Jesus' parable, can "come to ourselves" and "rise and go to our Father."

We do not have to stay in the pigsty. Randy Maddox aptly calls this "responsible grace" because God's grace requires our faith-filled response. In Jesus' parable of the prodigal son, the boy "comes to himself." He comes home from the "weeds" to the porch.

If we do respond to these "God whispers" positively, Wesley preached, "His eyes are opened in quite another manner than before, even to see a loving, gracious God." [115]

In his sermon, *The Spirit of Bondage and Adoption,* Wesley preaches,

---

115 Op. Cit., Outler, ed, Vol. 1, JWW, 260.

"By his Word applied with the demonstration of his Spirit, God touches the heart of him that lay asleep in darkness and in the shadow of death. He is shaken out of his sleep and awakes into a consciousness of his danger. Perhaps in a moment, perhaps by degrees, the eyes of his understanding are opened, and now discern the real state he is in." [116]

In this metaphor, do not think geographically; "coming home" may be from a geographic distance or in the same community! It is simply responding to the "God nudge." Wesley's message was intended to sensitize the person "dead in his sins," motivating him or her to hear the "whisper in the heart" of the Holy Spirit.

If, from the "hedges," we rise and approach "home where the candle is burning in the window," let us look more closely at Wesley's metaphor of the proverbial "homeplace." In that environment, children experienced love, security, precious memories, and Christian nurture. This meant nightly prayers, table grace, Sunday School every Sunday, manners, respect for elders, honesty in character, absence of profanity and alcohol, sportsmanship in athletics, kindness to ethnic minority persons, and sexual abstinence before marriage. It is to that they sing, "Lord, I'm coming home, never more to roam..."

Dr. Harry Emerson Fosdick, longtime pastor of Riverside Church in New York City, defined this as "like crossing a river – near the head of the stream where it requires only a small step across a brook, or at the mouth where it requires a long and arduous swim!" Because of the difference in life ages and stages when we come to Christ, the experience is different with each person.

Sadly, for some coming to Jesus is "a big wide river to cross." Religion was a stranger in their homes. Their "grounds" were neglected thickets of brambles and briars. Some lived, as children, what my rural culture called "a dog's life." Coming home from what Jesus metaphorically called "the

---

116 Ibid., 255.

far country" and kneeling on "Repentance Porch" is a journey "through many dangers, toils, and snares" for some.

An example of finding grace and coming home as a strange concept is seen poignantly in the life story of a friend of mine. His autobiography is entitled, *Castaway Kid.* It is an accurate title because when he was two, his mother took him to a strange place with some toys with which he began to play. He looked around and realized that his mother was gone. She had cast him away and he was now in an orphanage. As a teenager, he asked a counselor at the orphanage camp, "Why should 'I apologize' to a God who is not there for me and never has been?" [117] His prayer was, "Jesus, if you are real, come into my nightmare." [118]

Looking back to that prayer, Rob wrote years later, "Not exactly the kind of prayer that Billy Graham would have suggested. I didn't hear angels singing. I didn't fall down and roll around in spiritual ecstasy. But somehow I knew that the God of the universe had reached deep into my heart and something had changed. For the first time in years, I could not wait to see what was coming next in my life." [119] Biographies of outstanding persons from varied home backgrounds are filled with similar stories. When the "yard" is full of painful experiences, imagining love, mercy, and grace is very difficult.

We see this in Joseph Hart of the eighteenth century who described himself as "a boldfaced rebel." At church he heard only words of condemnation. Finally, at the age of forty-five, he heard words of hope in a Moravian chapel in London, and a bit later wrote these words as his spiritual journey. Christian mentors have often been the "angels" in children's or students' lives as they encouraged those who might be disenfranchised or disenchanted. Joseph Hart's words are for just such people:

> *"Come ye sinners, poor and needy, weak and wounded,*
> *sick and sore;*

---

117 Mitchell, Rob, *Castaway Kid*, Tyndale House, 2007, 133.

118 Ibid., 134.

119 Ibid. 134.

Jesus ready stands to save you, full of pity, love and power.

Come ye thirsty, come and welcome God's free bounty glorify.

True belief and true repentance every grace will bring you nigh.

Come ye weary, heavy laden, lost and ruin-éd by the fall;

If you tarry, till you're better, you will never come at all.

Let not conscience make you linger nor of fitness fondly dream;

All the fitness he requireth is to feel your need of Him."

Response:

"I will rise and go to Jesus; he will embrace me with his words;

In the arms of my dear Savior, There's relief from all alarms."

Whatever our journey, God loves us equally and, in the mystery of grace upon grace, God whispers to every heart in some way." To use again the language of Rafiki the mandrill to young Simba in *The Lion King:* "You are more than you have become."

Some, however, make their way out of the "hedges" alone. They simply follow what the Quakers and Catholic Father Richard Rohr call "the inner light." Whether fumbling, stumbling, or fulfilling the nurture of loving parents and a good church faith community, we make our way to what Wesley called the "porch of repentance."

The "Porch" of Repentance

In Wesley's metaphor, the "house of faith" has a porch that is "Repentance Porch." Whatever the nature and time of our journey since God nudged us, when we come to our porch, we are at the house, but not in the house. Now picture yourself.

From what kind of spiritual journey do you arrive at the "porch of repentance?" One thing we have in common when we fall onto the "porch": we are all sinners and need to repent of some combination of thoughts, words, or deeds that grieved God.

But what does it mean to repent? Unfortunately, many associate it with negative images:

- being pressured by Christians on campus to repeat after them some confession of sins
- kneeling at a church altar
- reaching the dead end of the consequences of bad decisions and bathing in a sense of failure
- privately groveling in guilt of something you did that cannot be undone

All that is more remorse than it is repentance. Remorse can lead to depression, despondency, and despair. It is a "woe is me" feeling with no sense of hope.

Repentance, in Greek, on the other hand, is the proactive word *metanoia,* which loosely translated means, "turning around and going the other way." Repentance involves change – in behavior, attitude, and habits of dependency and dysfunctional relationships. As Steve Harper puts it in his book, *John Wesley's Message for Today,* " Now we know that sin matters; it must be forsaken. As St. Paul put it, "All have sinned and fall short of the glory of God." (Romans 3:23 {NIV}) Each of us must come to terms with the truth of this passage. Wesley insisted that we must repent before we can have what he called a "heartfelt religion."

We have had enough narrow escapes with moral or ethical failure. We have enough scars from being controlled by our emotions or our hormones. We decide that the time has come for the catharsis of surrendering to God's guidance as best we understand it. If we are adults, this takes eating a sizable piece of "Humble Pie." The Holy Spirit needs to become "the steering wheel" guiding all our decisions, attitudes, and actions. So, it is that on the "porch of repentance," we covenant with God to change our lives.

In repentance, we first must ask God to forgive us of our sins that we have done and sins of what we have left undone. We call these "sins of commission and sins of omission." Whether our repentance has been for sins of the flesh or sins of the spirit, we are all sinners. This is "change time" regardless of our life to this point. Now we know that God matters; we shall follow Him. Tears may or may not be involved. Repentance also changes our will, our liberty of choice.

The knotty tangle of sin and guilt can be untied only by internalizing that Jesus died on the cross that we might have eternal life. We must be cut off from dependency upon ourselves, any substance, or any human relationship before we can truly depend on Christ. We must guard against a lockstep process and remember that Jesus met each person in accordance with her or his personality, life situation, and acute need. Jesus meets us where we are and as we are and whoever we are.

The decision to rise from "Repentance Porch" is the free will decision to take God's "helping hand" as one would grasp a rope for the way out of a dark cavern. The level and kind of emotion depends both on your emotional psyche and on your previous life.

One thing, though, is certain; the essence of repentance is a proactive, demonstrative change. William Abraham of the SMU faculty, says, "A helping hand enters into the deepest recesses of the human agent and redirects and re-engineers everything from top to bottom." [120]

Jesus said to the man beside the pool who had not walked in thirty-eight years, "Rise up and walk." Whatever our life situation, we need to make a "change covenant" with the Lord before we leave the "porch of repentance." So, just do it! Rise up and "walk through the threshold of grace." The Waiting Father has "seen you on the porch." Welcome home! The door is open. Are you ready now to step through the threshold of grace?

---

120 Op. Cit., Abraham, 79.

The Irish have a phrase called "thin place." This is a passage from one place or life season to another where we are still partially in what we left and partially in what we are entering. The threshold of a house is such a "thin place"; standing in it, we are half outside and half inside the house. So is the threshold of grace. In this "thin place," we are walking "by faith and not by sight." You are still wearing some of the regrets and scars of your past, but you are entering a new dimension of life – "your faith in God's saving grace." You are fragile. Paul speaks of our being a "babe in Christ" who can intake only "milk, not meat." We need the support of a church that is a caring faith community, or, like Alcoholics Anonymous, a "sponsor."

The Threshold of Grace

The "porch" of repentance is a necessary prelude to "victory in Jesus," but it is not a place to stay and stagnate. Far too many people regale hearers for years on the time, place, and emotions of their being saved. When you enter a home, you love an open door and a warm welcome, but you don't tarry in the threshold!

Christianity, according to John Wesley, is not a "solitary religion." Coming home to faith in God's grace also means a change in your relationships, even your most intimate relationships. Once through the threshold and into the house, you need to do something! This is either your new home or a new beginning with your family, friends, and colleagues. Texas oil business executive Keith Miller tells us his story in his autobiography, *Taste of New Wine.*

Rushing from a new oil well, he "heard" the voice of God, pulled his Mercedes over on a Texas roadside, and repented of his sins. He said that if he went home and told his wife he had become a Christian sitting in his Mercedes, she would be unimpressed. But since their honeymoon, she had expected him to take out the trash because her dad did, and he had for years refused, claiming it was "woman's work." That night when he arrived home, he opened the door under the sink, and took out the garbage! When he came in, she was in tears as she hugged him and asked what had happened. Taking out the garbage spoke much more loudly than his oral testimony would have!

Wesley's sermon, *The Spirit of Bondage and Adoption,* is helpful here. We know of at least thirty-one times of record that he preached from Romans 8:15. Wesley poignantly details the many people who are good, but live with "spiritual pain management" and without experiential grace:

"We often deceive ourselves because we do not consider how far a man may go and yet be in a natural, or at best a legal state. A man may be of a compassionate and benevolent temper; he may be affable, courteous, generous, friendly; he may have some degree of meekness, patience, temperance and many other moral virtues; he may feel many desires to shake off all vice and attain high degrees of virtue; he may abstain from much evil – perhaps all that is grossly contrary to justice, mercy, or truth; he may do much good, may feed the hungry, clothe the naked, relieve the widow and fatherless; he may attend public worship, use prayer in private, read many books of devotion – yet for all this he may be a mere natural man, knowing neither himself nor God; equally a stranger to the spirit of fear and to that of love; having neither repented nor believed the gospel." [121]

Then Wesley comes to his point: "Nay, God hath prepared better things for thee. Thou art not called to fear and tremble like devils do, but to rejoice and love like the angels of God. Thou shalt 'rejoice evermore.'" (I Thessalonians 5:16 {NIV}) To paraphrase Wesley's conclusion, he says, "Hold on to what you have now attained by "reaching forth to those things that are in your new future." He refers then to Philippians 3:13 {NIV} where Paul confesses and professes his own faith:

---

121 Op. Cit., Wesley, John, "Spirit of Bondage and Adoption," JWW, Vol. 1, 265-266.

"Brothers, I do not consider myself yet to have taken hold of it, but one thing I do: Forgetting what is behind and straining toward what is ahead, I press on toward the goal to win the prize for which God has called me heavenward in Christ Jesus."

Wesley's larger point in his sermon, *Spirit of Bondage and Adoption,* was that we need to sense God's releasing us from the bondage of doing good on our own strength and accepting what he calls "God's spirit of adoption." The text for this sermon is Paul's gracious words to the Romans: "For you did not receive a spirit that makes you a slave again to fear, but you have received the spirit of adoption, and by him, we cry, 'Abba,' 'Father.'" [122] (Romans 8:15 {NIV}) SO! You are now welcomed home as a new Christian! We shall return to Wesley's paradigm of the "house of salvation" in our chapter entitled, "Perfecting Grace" that is God's helping us to "clean house" with our attitudes, addictions, biases, prejudices, and other needs for God to do "spring cleaning" in our heads and hearts!

The Gist of the Gospel: John 3:16!

Get your Bible and read John 3:16. It is the essence of the Gospel. Walk through this paraphrase:

God loved the world, including me, so much

that God gave of himself (his only Son)

that whoever believes in Jesus ('whosoever surely means me')

will not perish ('waste away')

but have eternal ('abundant') life.

Many of us as children prayed a table grace that began: "God is great, God is good...." We have no problem believing that God is great; but considering the evil in the world, we have an issue with God's being good. In the book, *The Shack,* Mack

---

122 "Abba" was the familial word that Palestinian children used to address their father in Jesus' day.

cannot move from repentance to trusting in God in the aftermath of Mack's little daughter's murder. God says to Mack:

"The real underlying flaw in your life, Mackenzie, is that you don't think I am good. If you knew I was good and that everything – the means, the ends, and all the processing of individual life events – is all covered by my goodness, then while you might not always understand what I am doing, you would trust me. Trust is the fruit of a relationship in which you know you are loved. Until you know I love you, you cannot trust me." [123]

A major roadblock in trusting God and having faith is just what William Young said–a question about the character of God's goodness and love. As Steve Harper points out, it was the "prodigal son's trust in his father's love that gave him the confidence to go home." [124] Sadly, the Calvinists and cultural theology have made us believe in God's sovereignty and power as pre-empting God's love.

It is God's grace, not our faith, that saves us. Contemporary Christian songwriter, Chris Tomlin, has recorded a modern version of the most popular hymn in America that illustrates being forgiven, accepting Jesus as Savior, and walking through the threshold of grace:

"Amazing grace how sweet the sound that saved a wretch like me;

I once was lost, but now am found; was blind but now I see.

My chains are gone; I've been set free; My God, my Savior ransomed me.

And like a flood, his mercy reigns; unending love, amazing grace."

You might have sometime seen the painting of Jesus knock-

---

123 Op. Cit, Young, 126.

124 Op. Cit., Harper, 55.

ing at the door of our heart. Holman Hunt painted that and it hangs in St. Paul's Cathedral in London. Entitled, "Christ at the Door," it so beautifully portrays God's seeking love. He was inspired by Revelation 3:20 and an old abandoned building in the Trossach Mountains. Vines were growing on the door from years of neglect. It reminded him of his own life!

There is no latch; Christ is knocking at the door, but with the latch on the inside, the occupant can leave the door closed or can open it. The Revelation text reads, "Here I am! I stand at the door and knock. If anyone hears my voice and opens the door, I will come in, and eat with him and he with me." (The Message) As we have written before, grace is synergistic; you must respond positively for Jesus to come into your heart and life.

In John 3:16, God did his part – God gave His only son! Now John clearly states "whoever believes will not perish." However, "not perishing" is only avoiding the dark side.

The bright side is, "but have eternal life."

So John 3:16 {NIV} contains the essence of the Christian gospel: God gave his utmost that we must have life more abundantly here and hereafter. Beautiful!

Leonard Sweet has a marvelous gift for expressing things in a novel, intriguing way. He describes the new birth and eternal life in what he has coined as a *Letter from God:*

A Letter from God

"When you received my Son, you are born a second time and from a different realm. You were born 'from above.' Don't be surprised (as Nicodemus was) when I say you are 'born from above.' Birth is the impartation of life. In your natural birth you were born of corruptible seed, but when you were born again, an incorruptible seed of My Life was placed into you by My Spirit.

In I Peter 1:23, we read, 'You have been born anew, not of

114

perishable but of imperishable seed, through the living and enduring Word of God. That seed was Christ who became a new dimension of your DNA. This new life is what Jesus called "eternal life." Eternal life does not point to longevity in heaven, but a new quality of an extraordinary life. This is what Jesus imparts when he says, 'I am the resurrection and the life.' In I John we read, 'We know the Son of God has come and given us an understanding that we may know Him who is true, and we are in Him who is true. He is the true God and eternal life." [125] (I John 5:11-12, 20 {NIV})

So it is that salvation is not a prescribed plan. Rather, it is a relationship, entered into incrementally or instantaneously. Just as the relationship of a parent who has more than one child is different with each child, God's children each has a personal relationship with our heavenly Father. Some come to saving grace through incremental nurture, some come through their conviction about social injustices, some come through a need for personal inner peace with God during a crisis or advanced season of life.

John the Elder wrote for us, "If we walk in the light as he is in the light, we have fellowship with one another...." (I John 1:7 {NIV}) My mother used to say of some Christians who were deeply prejudiced, "They are walking in all the light that they have." Would to God that we could all be that charitable with our Christian fellow pilgrims who differ from us.

Wesley's Paradigm of "therapeutic grace"

Wesley was a widely read professor before he was a preacher. He knew like the palm of his hand the theology of the early church prior to Augustine, Augustine's theology, (354-430 C.E) and the Eastern Orthodox Church theology after Augustine. This is so important because Augustine attributed our salvation only to Jesus' atoning death on the cross. Most of us still state our belief in that paradigm, "I am a Christian because Jesus died in my place for my sins." That is, I deserve the death

---

125 Op. Cit, Sweet and Viola, 44-45.

sentence, but Jesus volunteered to die in my place. That is the paradigm of the court and the language of the judge and plaintiff. John Wesley was drawn, though, to the paradigm of Eastern Christianity – the Church in the lands to which Paul wrote most of his letters – Galatia, Colossae, Ephesus, Thessalonica, Philippi, and Corinth. Those Christians attribute our salvation to both the Crucifixion and the Incarnation. John in his Gospel wrote, "The true light that gives light to every man was coming into the world. The Word became flesh and lived among us, and made his dwelling among us. We have seen his glory, the glory of the One and Only, who came from the Father, full of grace and truth." (John 1:9,14, 16 {NIV}) As Bishop Athanasius of Alexandria put it, "God became like us so that we might become more like God."

While we are in the theological lineage of the Catholic Church, we do need to pay more heed to the "light from the East!" They see the need in salvation to enable us to recover the Likeness of God.

To the Eastern Orthodox Christians, this means to be freed from our slavery to sin and empowered by the restored Presence of God, the work of the Holy Spirit. Eastern Christianity exalted the consequence of Jesus' resurrection. They believe that Jesus' crucifixion was the last and damnable work of humanity, but that the resurrection was the subsequent and healing work of God. Therefore, in being saved, we are provided not just a "stay out of hell card," but a spiritual healing for what Jesus promised as abundant life and what we experience as renewable growth in grace.

We are deeply indebted to Dr. Randy Maddox of Duke Divinity School for emphasizing this therapeutic paradigm in Wesley's teachings and that they are anchored in Jesus' teachings. He documents that Wesley saw sin as a dis-ease for which only God has the remedy. Wesley and Arminius saw salvation in clinical, therapeutic terms – being healed from the dis-ease of sin.[126] If we think "spiritual clinic" rather than "court adju-

---

126 Op. Cit., Maddox, *Responsible Grace,* 121, 144-145, paraphrased.

dication," we can see Jesus as the Great Physician healing the "sin-sick soul and making the wounded whole" instead of his being our defense attorney before a judge.

Jesus and Wesley saw salvation more therapeutically than juridically. Wesley called being saved, "taking the cure." Being a Christian is more like going to the doctor rather than going to court! Maddox insists that Wesley's preference for the work of the Spirit is "healing."

In his sermon, "Plain Account of Primitive Christianity," Wesley used the phrase, "the renewal of our souls after the image of God." Therefore, like that of Eastern Christianity, Wesley's desire is for God's grace to empower us with a recovery of the likeness of God (progressive realization of that potentiality). To accomplish this, we need to be freed from the power of sin and empowered by the Presence of God. A corollary of this is the emphasis of God's love more than God's sense of justice.

Though therapy is never an accomplished fact, but a healing process, the emphasis on healing is so much in sync with Jesus' ministry. Jesus' "Sermon on the Mount" enunciates a "higher happiness." We can move to that spiritual higher ground if by faith we begin to see God as a sovereign power who really cares.

Seeing saving grace as having a therapeutic cure is not a new discovery with recent Methodist theologians. We see this same theme in two old gospel hymns. One was a favorite of my mother's:

"The great Physician now is here, the sympathizing Jesus

He speaks the drooping heart to cheer, O hear the voice of Jesus..."

Another hymn that was constantly requested in my first parish is, *"Does Jesus Care?"* In my first parish, Isaac Dennis was brought each Sunday from the local sanatorium where he was a perennial patient for tuberculosis. He was thin and frail. Whenever in that small church I asked people to request a hymn, we knew what Isaac would request and why. The hymn was written by a minister whose own troubles were inspired for healing when he read I Peter 5:7 {NIV}, "Cast all your anxieties on him because he cares for you." Identifying with Isaac, we all sang from our hearts:

> *"Does Jesus care when my heart is pained too deeply for mirth or song,*
>
> *As the burdens press and the cares distress and the way grows weary and long?*
>
> *Does Jesus care when my way is dark with nameless dread and fear?*
>
> *As the daylight fades into deep night shades, does He care enough to be near?*
>
> *Does Jesus care when I've said 'goodbye' to the dearest on earth to me,*
>
> *And my sad heart aches 'til it nearly breaks, is it aught to Him? Does He see?*
>
> *Refrain:*
>
> *O yes, He cares, I know he cares; his heart is touched with my grief;*
>
> *When the days are weary and the long nights dreary, I know my Savior cares."*

We see this "caring" theme rather than a "court of judgment theme" in one of the most well-known and often sung gospel hymns:

> *"What a friend we have in Jesus, all our sins and griefs to bear,*
>
> *What a privilege to carry everything to him in prayer.*
>
> *Do thy friends despise, forsake thee? Is there trouble anywhere?*
>
> *In his arms he'll take and shield thee, thou wilt find a*

solace there."

In Jesus, and only in Jesus, do we see the perfect portrait of God. God's dominant attribute is love. Jesus did not die to "buy" our forgiveness, but to demonstrate God's love for us whether we have lost our way spiritually, or are hurting emotionally. Jesus' mission was to empower us to practice this gospel. If we believe God is love, we can sense Jesus' arms of mercy and pardon as we "hear" his words, "Come to me, all you who are weary and burdened, and I will give you rest, for I am gentle and humble in heart, and you will find rest for your souls. For my yoke is easy and my burden is light." (Matthew 11:28-30 {NIV})

According again to Randy Maddox, Wesley's was a "relational anthropology. As we become "in Christ," we love and enjoy and obey God, lovingly and caringly serve people, are stewards of nature, protect animals, and consequently, move out of guilt, shame, fear, doubt, and other dimensions of dis-ease to become healthy emotionally and spiritually.[127] Wesley said, "There is no holiness but social holiness." Or as the poet, John Donne, put it,

"No man is an island...Every man is a piece of a continent... if a clod be washed into the sea, Europe is the less.... Any man's death diminishes me because I am involved in mankind, and therefore never send to know for whom the bell tolls; it tolls for thee." [128]

Faith, in Wesley's language, is more than "good living," more than feeling, and more than doctrine. It is "a sure trust and confidence that Christ died for my sins, that God loves me." We must remember that for Wesley, God's "way of salvation" is anchored in God's character – love. In order to trust him, we must internalize this and it is hard to do!

He repeatedly summarized his creed in the words Jesus used to summarize the law and the prophets: "Thou shalt love the Lord thy God with all thy mind, soul, and strength, and love

127 Ibid. 68.

128 Donne, John, *Sermon #75 preached to the Earl of Carlisle*, c. 1622.

thy neighbor as thyself." (Luke 10:27 {NIV})

Charlotte Elliott was an invalid who was bitter to the point that no nurse could care for her very long. Then she made this leap of faith and wrote about it in lyrics that have called millions to a similar experience. Her words, like her life journey to faith, had a therapeutic accent:

"Just as I am, though tossed about with many a conflict, many a doubt,

Fightings and fears within, without, O Lamb of God I come, I come.

Just as I am, poor, wretched, blind; sight, riches, healing of the mind,

Yea, all I need in thee I'll find, O Lamb of God I come, I come.

Just as I am thou wilt receive, will welcome, pardon, cleanse, relieve.

Because thy promise I believe, O Lamb of God, I come, I come."

The truth is that most people are like "Pilgrim" in the classic, *Pilgrim's Progress,* coming to a place in his journey that he calls "Interpreter's House."

These are our "God moments." We need in every church with great frequency in the pulpit, in small groups, and in material like this book to help people interpret their "God moments." It is liberating as Jesus says what no other master will say: "My yoke is easy and my burden is light. I am come that you might have a more abundant life." (Matthew 11:30 {NIV}) As every person, seeker or "old" Christian, senses the "call of the Deep," we need to help them learn to pray, "Jesus, Savior, pilot me over life's tempestuous sea."

Bottom line: being saved is coming home, entering the threshold of grace, feeling forgiven, feeling cared for, feeling loved. Being loved has several therapeutic dimensions: to be restored, healed, and quietly confident that you and I are a son or daughter of the most high God whom you now call, "Abba, Father." At age eighty-three, I can say with authority that every season of life brings new challenges to our faith in God's grace. Therefore, our journey must be as Mr. Wesley so picturesquely described it: "grace upon grace."

Questions for Discussion and Reflection

This chapter is crucial to anyone's faith journey who is a seeker or who is questioning her/his faith experience. Did you find it helpful? Could you lift this chapter alone out of this book and give it to someone giving evidence that their "soul is being awakened?"

Can you personally say, "I have been born again?" (Do not take this to mean you have to point to a moment or place).

Do you think everyone at one time or another feels the "whisper of the Holy Spirit" that can lead to an "awakening of the soul," as Wesley called it? Have you had such moments?

Think about or discuss some differing paths on which we come to our personal faith.

Did you note the difference between remorse and repentance?

Do you believe we can backslide? If so, you are not a Calvinist!

Do you believe God's saving grace is for all and we can accept or reject it? If so, you are not a Calvinist!

If we don't love ourselves at this point in our journey, it is hard to believe that the holy God loves us. Can you believe that? Everything else in becoming a Christian or remaining a Christian rests on the premise that our behavior does not identify us–we are a child of God regardless of behavior and that is our identity. Sign your name on a card you keep in your wallet:

I, _____, (son/daughter) of the Most High God, affirm that I am made in His Image, and am redeemable by his Love.

I believe that God loves me just as I am. I this day have repented of my sins and am ready to walk through the door of the "threshold of grace" and accept Jesus as my Savior from sin and the Lord of my daily decisions and eternal destiny.

_____
Signature

_____
Date

Chapter Seven

Baptism–What Happens?
Reflection on Baptism as a Sacrament

First of all, let us distinguish between the occasion of each of our two sacraments.

The Eucharist, or Holy Communion, is to be received communally by the whole congregation and it is to be received repetitively.

On the other hand, baptism is to be received individually and initiates the baptized person by name into the Body of Christ. Since you cannot be initiated but once, baptism is non-repetitive.[129] To be re-baptized is to regard one's first baptism as null and void – an insult of the highest order to the Church that administered the holy sacrament in good faith.

Ironically, there is no biblical mention of the Twelve Apostles' ever being baptized! However, in the Great Commission, Jesus called for baptism as the new faith was spread around the world. (Matthew 28:16-20 {NIV})

In the twentieth century, Karl Barth thundered, "The Church did not invent Baptism, but administers it as it has been instituted by her Lord. It is Christ himself who made water baptism powerful. He did not need this for himself. Rather, he was baptized to declare his solidarity with sinner just as he was

---

129 Cullman, Oscar, *Baptism in the New Testament*, SCM Press, 1961, 29.

crucified on the cross." [130]

The sacrament in the Book of Acts has at its heart the faith that was centered in the death and resurrection of Jesus Christ, baptism by water, and a new covenant between God and the baptized that is ratified in the seal of the Spirit.

The great conflicts between denominations have been both on the meaning of baptism and the mode of baptism. There is scriptural support for all three modes – sprinkling, pouring, and immersion. All modes are symbols of God's love and the presence of the Holy Spirit; the amount of water has no significance. Therefore, the baptism of all Christian churches should be reciprocal.

Baptism in the New Testament

In preparation of the theological statement for the 1972 *United Methodist Book of Discipline,* Dr. Albert Outler coined a phrase that John Wesley never used – the word "quadrilateral." Outler said that every doctrine should get a four-way test:

1) Is it scriptural?

2) Is it traditional?

3) Is it reasonable?

4) Is it experienced?"

In 1988, this was revised to insist that of the four criteria, Scripture was primary. Since Scripture is primary, let us ask anew, "What does the New Testament say about baptism, and, especially, infant baptism?"

First, let's examine the modes of baptism:

Sprinkling

Sprinkling came from the Jews. In the Old Testament, we read, "I will sprinkle clean water on you and you will be clean...." (Ezekiel 36:25 {NIV}) The weed "hyssop" was often used

---

130 Barth, Karl, The Knowledge of God and the Service of God, Hodder and Stoughton, 1933, 211.

to sprinkle the water. Sprinkling is from logistical convenience, like the baptism of Cornelius and his household, the Philippian jailer and his household in the jail at midnight, and the baptism of Lydia and her whole family. Sprinkling also is the mode most conducive to spontaneous requests for baptism as in a military setting, ICU in a hospital, or on one's death bed. In those real life situations, the modes of sprinkling or pouring are the only options except to refuse baptism to the gravely ill or dying person.

Pouring

Pouring, which technically is "affusion," comes from the biblical account of the Day of Pentecost. In the first Christian sermon ever preached, Peter said, "God has raised this Jesus to life, and we are all witnesses of the fact. Exalted to the right hand of God, he has received from the Father the promised Holy Spirit and has poured out what you now see and hear." (Acts 2:32-33 {NIV}) Luke, the author of the Book of Acts, then tells us that immediately, "Those who accepted his message were baptized, and about three thousand were added to their number that day." (Acts 2:41 {NIV}) Considering that the followers of Jesus were virtual outlaws, that Jerusalem had only three pools, and that there were only eleven disciples, most scholars think that the Pentecost baptisms were by pouring or sprinkling.

Immersion

Immersion was obviously practiced in the early church because baptisteries have been uncovered by archaeologists. This mode was associated with Jesus' baptism by John in the Jordan River. The favorite scripture verse for it is Paul's reference in Romans 6:3-4 {NIV}: "Don't you know that all of us who were baptized into Christ Jesus were baptized into his death? We were therefore buried with him through baptism into death in order that, just as Christ was raised from the dead...we too may live a new life." (Scholars who are not bound to the mode of immersion interpret this as a reference to the cross and Jesus' death; nevertheless, this is the favorite "proof text" of those who baptize only by immersion.)

Most Bible commentators, including United Methodists, look at New Testament references to baptism through their own doctrinal bias. We shall draw the position of this book on the theology of baptism in the New Testament, not from denominational tradition, per se.

Among New Testament scholars, none has done more important work than Oscar Cullman. A German Lutheran, Cullman's work has been used by all Protestants and by the Roman Catholic Church under three popes. His small but wonderfully researched works were major references in all outstanding seminaries in the 1950's. From 1938 until 1972 he was Professor of New Testament and Early Church History at the University of Basel. After 1949 he was also adjunct faculty at the Sorbonne in Paris and was regarded with highest esteem in the United Kingdom and the United States. Unfortunately, his works are not used in seminaries today as much as they were in the 1940's and 1950's. He died in 1999 when he was still writing at the age of ninety-six!

In 1961, he wrote an enormously helpful and scripturally based book, *Baptism in the New Testament.* Perhaps no one else has explained the term "baptismal regeneration" so helpfully. Dr. Cullman began his chapter entitled "Baptism and Faith" with this profound insight:

"Baptism involved two things: 1) What happens at the moment when baptismal action takes place? and, 2) On the other hand, "what results from Baptism extend through the whole life of the person baptized? The complete baptismal event is composed of not less than both of these together." [131]

---

131 Op. Cit., Cullman 47.

Jesus' Baptism by John

What was the meaning of Jesus' baptism by John the Baptist? What relation is the meaning of Jesus' baptism to our baptism since he was without sin and we are sinners?

The first baptism mentioned in the New Testament was the baptism of Jesus by John the Baptist (more accurately, "John the baptizer"). Yet, as World Council of Churches staff scholar, Robert Paul, has written, "we cannot imagine that our Lord as a baby demanded to be circumcised or made a willful decision to be. It was a responsibility which his human parents, out of their own faith and piety undertook for him: 'On the eighth day when it was time to circumcise him, he was named Jesus, the name the angel had given him before he had been conceived. ... Joseph and Mary took him to Jerusalem to present him to the Lord.'" [132] (Luke 2:21-23 {NIV})

His parents did this for him. So, in circumcision we see the finger of God's choice laid upon him without his rational consent (at eight days old). When blind old Simeon took the child on the day of his circumcision and dedication, he said, "For my eyes have seen your salvation...a light for revelation to the Gentiles and for glory to your people Israel." (Luke 2:30-32 {NIV}) Luke concluded the nativity with the words, "And Jesus grew in wisdom, and stature, and favor with God and man." We see, as a boy in the Temple and a man at his baptism, our Lord consciously and willingly accepting his mission as the Son of God that would lead to the Cross." [133]

Before the baptism of Jesus, Judaism already practiced the external act of water baptism for Gentiles who converted. God prophesied through Ezekiel, "I will sprinkle clean water on you and you will be clean; I will cleanse you from your impurities...I will give you a new heart and put a new spirit in you." (Ezekiel 36:25-26 {NIV}) Baptism by immersion is not mentioned in the Old Testament, but it probably was the mode practiced by

---

132 Paul, Robert, *The Atonement and the Sacraments*, Abingdon, 1960, 329.

133 Ibid., 329.

the Essene community by the Dead Sea.

Jesus was baptized by John in the Jordan not as a repenting sinner, but as God's Son being baptized for mission. The voice of the Holy Spirit from heaven, not the water, was the confirmation of Jesus' being the Son of God, "commissioned" for a servant ministry.

Neither the Jews before John the Baptist, nor John himself, baptized except with water, but John said, "The one coming after me will baptize with the Holy Spirit." (Mark 1:8 {NIV}) It is valid to point out that John's was a Jewish baptism, not a Christian one, but most importantly, as Dr. Paul insists, "Christ's Sonship was acknowledged in the context of Jesus' freedom, or his willingness to take on the mission of the Son." [134] Jesus voluntarily accepted his mission on earth, not as predestined fate, but as a call to "fulfill the law."

In Jesus' baptism, the gift of the Spirit was infinitely more important than the amount of water. Water baptism was obviously not a hallmark of Jesus' own ministry. Some wag has said that when the crowd heard the voice, "God was saying, 'YES! That's my boy.'") It is the Holy Spirit, not the mode, that should be emphasized in baptism.

According to Professor Oscar Cullman, Jesus' baptism in the Jordan has three meanings: [135]

Our Lord's voluntary acceptance of his destiny was not as "fate" but as mission. Forgiveness of sin is not forgiveness of Jesus' sins, but was in effect a general and vicarious forgiveness for the sins of the whole world. His baptism anticipated the cross (Mark 10:38; Luke 12:50 {NIV}) as the 'suffering servant' passages in Isaiah 53 {NIV}. His baptism was to die; yet the voice from heaven distinguished him as the Messiah, a conception impossible for Judaism.

---

134 Ibid. 332.

135 Op. Cit., 14-15.

Jesus' baptism locked together forever the forgiveness of sin and coming of the Spirit.

The essence of baptism is that it is Christ who is the redeeming operative while the person being baptized is the object of Christ's deed. "Tis done!"

Jesus' teaching about children's place in the Kingdom of Heaven

Though Jesus did not mention baptism, his words about children are profoundly inclusive:

> "People were bringing even infants to him that he might touch them; and when the disciples saw it, they sternly ordered them not to do it. But Jesus called for them and said, 'Let the little children come to me and do not stop them; for it is to such as these that the kingdom of God belongs. Truly I tell you, whoever does not receive the kingdom of God as a little child will never enter it.'"
>
> **Matthew 19:14 (NIV)**

John Calvin used this verse as what he called "a defense against the Anabaptists." [136] Certainly, this occasion, recorded in Matthew, Mark, and Luke, did not refer to baptism, per se, but no serious scholar ever proposed that the early church invented the occurrence to provide scriptural authority for baptizing infants, a practice that was almost universal by 200 C.E. It is Jesus' blessing and the laying on of hands, not water baptism, but the key phrase is "forbid them not." Infant baptism is a celebration of the theological principle enunciated by Jesus – if children have a place in the Kingdom of God, they have a place in the church!

---

136 Benoit, J. D. *"Calvin et le baptême des enfants,"* in the *Revue d'Histoire et de Philosophie religieuses,* 1937, 263.

The New Testament connection between Water Baptism and Baptism of the Holy Spirit

The first Christian baptism was following Pentecost, fifty days after Jesus resurrection. The Holy Spirit that accompanied Jesus at his baptism is now manifested to the new converts who would constitute the new church! Again, the theological importance was the "pouring out of the Holy Spirit," not the water baptism. In language similar to that of John the Baptist at Jesus' baptism, Peter's invitation was, "Repent and be baptized every one of you, in the name of Jesus Christ for the forgiveness of your sins. And you will receive the gift of the Holy Spirit." (Acts 2:38 {NIV})

The apostles, who were not baptized themselves, felt the need of adding to the external act of baptism the laying on of hands as the symbol of the gift of the Holy Spirit. The Holy Spirit is in tandem with the water. This established an irrefutable biblical connection between the forgiveness of sins and the gift of the Holy Spirit.[137] We see this immediately after Pentecost when Philip baptized both men and women in Samaria: "Peter and John placed their hands on them and they received the Holy Spirit." (Acts: 8:17 {NIV}) We see this again with Paul's ministry in Ephesus: "Did you receive the Holy Spirit when you believed? 'No. We have not even heard that there is a Holy Spirit.'" (Acts 19:2 {NIV}) "When Paul placed hands on them, the Holy Spirit came on them...." (Acts 19:6 {NIV})

Indeed, Paul wrote, "...those who are led by the Spirit of God are sons of God." (Romans 8:14 {NIV}) He followed this with, "In the same way, the Spirit helps us in our weakness. We do not know what we ought to pray for, but that the Spirit intercedes for us with sighs that words cannot express" (Romans 8:26 {NIV}). To the Corinthians he wrote, "The Spirit searches everything, even the deep things of God." (I Cor. 2:10b {NIV}) A bit later in that letter he wrote, "...no one can say 'Jesus is Lord' except by the Holy Spirit." In this, the divine power was in the divine "pouring of the Spirit," not in the belief of the recipients.

---

137 Op. Cit., Cullman, 11.

God gave; they "received."

Professor Oscar Cullman wrote, "The death and resurrection of Christ is the centre of Baptism. Thus the baptismal death of Christ completed once for all on the cross passes over into Church Baptism!" [138]

Spirit baptism eclipsed water baptism.

The logistics are not favorable for immersion at the Pentecost mass baptism. Baptizing three thousand in Jerusalem only fifty days after the crucifixion would be improbable. There were only eleven disciples and no Deacons at that point in time. Each disciple would have had 272.7 converts to baptize! That would have drawn a crowd! Consider that both the Jews and the Romans were searching diligently for Jesus' followers. Would they have allowed long queues at the precious few pools in Jerusalem? No one expects to convince other Christian denominations to the contrary, but circumstantial evidence points away from the mode of immersion.

What about the least used mode – pouring? Pentecost itself is the occasion when Peter told the throng, "Exalted to the right hand of God, he has received from the Father the promised Holy Spirit, and has poured out what you now see and hear." (Acts 2:32-33 {NIV}) Methodist scholars have pointed out that since Pentecost is the first Christian baptism, if we are to symbolize literally the coming of the Holy Spirit, then "pouring" is the mode of baptism that most accurately portrays the descending Spirit! It is too seldom used!

St. Paul "on baptism"

Most New Testament references to baptism are in Paul's letters. Although we have the record of his baptism by Ananias in Damascus, (Acts 20:16 {NIV}) the emphasis of Paul's missionary ministry was on a faith-centered theology, not a sacramentarian theology. The final seat of authority for St. Paul seems to rest on the experience of being "in Christ" more than on the

---

[138] Ibid. 22.

sacrament of baptism. He was an itinerant preacher, a church
planter, and an inspired writer, not primarily a baptizer. He
specifically said, "For Christ did not send me to baptize, but
to preach the gospel...." (I Corinthians 1:17 {NIV}) He first said to
the Corinthians that he had baptized no one, but reluctantly
recalled that he did baptize Crispus, Gaius, and Stephanus (all
Greeks!). However, in his other epistles Paul did make numerous references to the baptism of converts.

Most of Paul's references to baptism referred to either
converts from paganism or from Judaism. With the exception
of Lydia (Acts 16:11-15 {NIV}) and the Roman jailer (Acts 16:25-40 {NIV}),
Paul's references were to adults. Except for these instances, all
New Testament baptisms were for adults: "Baptism was much
more than an intellectual assent; it included repentance from
one's sin, and a commitment to follow Jesus' route to the cross
with the assurance of resurrection." [139] Paul used the term
"baptized into Christ" which, according to Robert Paul and
others, implies a doctrine of baptismal regeneration at the time a
new convert was baptized 'into Christ.'

What the term "baptismal regeneration" means in its early church setting

Most all biblical interpreters agree that baptism was one's
initiation into the Church. In the Church as the nurturing faith
community, the Holy Spirit completes the miracle of a "life
change." If the awakened and repenting person being baptized
had not been baptized as an infant, the baptism would follow
a profession of faith. If the new convert had been baptized as
an infant or small child, the believer would not be re-baptized.
Rather, the profession of faith would lead to confirmation,
membership vows, and a lifelong journey of perfecting grace.
All this is possible, not by our willpower or self control but as
a gift of the Holy Spirit. So, it is that God's regenerating grace
begins with our baptism, is celebrated when we accept Christ as
our personal Savior and Lord, and continues all along our life

---

139 Op. Cit.,, Paul, reflections from Chapter X, 319-335.

journey, grace upon grace. St. Paul put it this way: "Continue to work out your salvation with fear and trembling for it is God who works in you enabling you to will and to act according to his good pleasure." (Philippians 2:12b-13 {NIV})

A brief history of the modes of Baptism

In the New Testament, most persons who received baptism were adults who were pagans or Jews that converted to Christianity. United Methodism, with a spiritual lineage from Catholicism through the Anglican Church, has always baptized infants. Is there scriptural justification for baptizing babies as a "sign-act" of grace? To be honest, there are no references to individuals who were baptized as infants. However, there is circumstantial evidence of infant baptism. In three instances, baptism was extended to "the family," the "whole house," or the "household":

Peter baptized the Gentile convert, Cornelius, "and his entire household" after Peter's vision had convinced him that "God does not show favoritism." (Acts 10:34 {NIV})

Lydia was a merchant in Thyatira, Greece. When she and her household were baptized, she invited Paul and Silas to stay in her home. Most scholars think she hosted a "house church." (Acts 16:11-15 {NIV})

When the earthquake occurred while Paul and Silas were in a house jail in Philippi, the jailer "seeing the doors open, drew a sword to kill himself, but Paul cried out, 'Do yourself no harm; we are all here.' Then the jailer called for lights, and sprang in and trembling, fell on his knees and...said, 'Sirs, what must I do to be saved?'" Paul interpreted his question spiritually: "'Believe in the Lord Jesus and thou shalt be saved, and thy household. And they spake the word of the Lord to all that were in his house.' And taking them that very hour of the night he washed their stripes and was immediately baptized, he and all his household" (Acts 16:30, 33b {NIV}).[140] Roman jails would not

---

140 Wesley, John, *Explanatory Notes Upon the New Testament*, Epworth Press, 2000, 461.

have afforded prisoners the comforts of a bathtub! They were likely sprinkled or "poured."

Most likely some or all of these families would have included children and could well have included infants. The major emphasis made in Paul's ministry, in John Wesley's ministry, and in Jesus' ministry was not water baptism but the presence of the Holy Spirit.

Secondly, nearly two hundred years before the Christian Church adopted our present twenty-seven books of the New Testament as the inspired canon, the bishops had begun to baptise infants! Even before Emperor Constantine made Christianity the "state church" of the Roman Empire, Bishop Iraneus (c. 135-202 C.E.) affirmed his baptizing infants in Lyon.[141]

The Catholic Church from the third century has practiced universal infant baptism. When King Henry VIII took the Anglican Church out of Catholicism, he continued infant baptism. When Martin Luther inspired the Protestant Reformation and ceased many Catholic practices, he continued infant baptism. Ulrich Zwingli in Zurich, broke with Luther and believed the Lord's Supper to be only a memorial meal. However, he retained infant baptism and prompted the city council to order all unbaptized babies to be presented for baptism within eight days.[142] That edict prompted the origin of what is called the "Anabaptist" movement.

The first Christian group to consider infant baptism as unscriptural was January 21, 1525 in a little Swiss town just south of the German border. For two years, they had been studying the scriptures and came to doubt the biblical justification for infant baptism. Reared as Catholics, all of them had been baptized at birth. On that night, though, one who was a married ex-priest asked another who was a layman, to re-baptize him. About fifteen others followed him that evening; they were baptized by "pouring," not immersion. The name the movement acquired was "Anabaptist" and they spread from Switzerland to

---

141 Op. Cit Cullman, 28.

142 Op. Cit., Walker, Williston, *A History of the Christian Church*, Scribner, 1985, 448.

Germany to Moravian in the Czech Republic. All were Calvinist in theology and all were pacifists. Many were executed, some in the most horrible of ways like public drowning by forced immersion while townspeople cheered. All Amish and Mennonites trace their religious heritage to these continental Anabaptists.

The Baptists in America trace their origins to John Smyth, an Anglican clergyman whose study of the Bible convinced him that baptism should be only for those who professed belief in Christ, repented of their sins, and wanted to be baptized by "pouring." Smyth baptized himself! He led his congregation to separate from the Church of England; so they were called "Separatists." A second congregation in northern England was established at Scrooby, and, John Robinson, the layman leading those "Separatists," took them to Amsterdam. They went back to England where they were called "General Baptists." They were Arminians because they believed Jesus died for all humanity, not just the elect. They were champions of religious toleration and separation of church and state. We know the rest of the story! They sailed on the Mayflower to America in 1620 and are known in American history as "Pilgrims."

The Puritans, who in 1640 followed the Pilgrims, were Calvinists. They practiced infant baptism, and did not believe in either religious toleration or separation of church and state. It was Roger Williams, who was about to be executed in Boston, who escaped and founded the first Baptist Church in America in the town he named "Providence" in the state he called Rhode Island. It is to Williams that American Baptists, and most colonial constitutions, owe our heritage of religious freedom and separation of church and state.

We indulge in this church history to illustrate the convoluted heritage of infant baptism. As we documented, only churches that trace their doctrinal roots to the Anabaptist movement in Switzerland and England oppose infant baptism. However, it is the variants of the Baptist churches, the rapidly growing independent church movement, and campus parachurch groups who insist that the only valid Christian baptism

135

is "believer's baptism." Most Christians see God's grace as the meaning of baptism. If the candidate's faith is the meaning, it cannot include God's babies. Therefore, Christians who were baptized as infants and reared in the Church and in Christian homes experience the heartache of seeing their loved ones' baptisms, in effect, declared "null and void." This breaks the hearts of parents and grandparents whose heritage in those churches have baptized their babies for generations. Family heirloom baptismal gowns made with loving hands and having the initials of the baptized children embroidered in the hems are mocked by non-use.

Infant Baptism

For those of us who affirm the biblical validity of infant baptism, what is the theological meaning? What happens when an infant is baptized?

The "Great Commission" in the closing verses of the Gospel of Matthew records Jesus having challenged his followers in every generation: "Therefore go and make disciples of all nations, baptizing them in the name of the Father, and of the Son, and of the Holy Spirit." (Matthew 28:19 {NIV}) However, no criteria are provided in scripture. We must ask, "Who was to be baptized and 'what happens' when one is baptized?" Except for three "family baptisms," all recorded baptisms in the Bible were adults who came as converted pagans or Jews.

In that context, we agree with Dr. Robert Paul: "Christian Baptism effects not simply cleansing – here it is in contrast to John's baptism of Jesus – but regeneration through faith in the redeeming work of Christ." [143] The baptism of the new convert could only be baptism 'into the Name' of Jesus Christ himself. This was far more than the intellectual acceptance of what Jesus had done; it was, in Paul's words, being "baptized into Christ." [144] Baptismal "regeneration," then, assumes a measure of moral accountability and spiritual perception that the infant

---

143 Op. Cit., Paul 339.

144 Ibid., 335.

does not have. So why, by the year 200 C.E., did the entire Christian Church begin baptizing infants and continue until January 21, 1525 in a small Swiss village?

The Church looked closely at Jesus' saying, "Let the children come to me and do not hinder them" (Matthew 19:14 {NIV}). The Church also was convinced that the terms "whole family" or "whole household" included the baptism of all the children, whatever their ages. The circumstantial evidence was that whole families were baptized when the "head of the family" became a Christian. Thereafter, that home would be a Christian home and the proverb would be fulfilled, "Train up a child in the way he should go, and when he is old, he will not turn from it." (Proverbs 22:6 {NIV})

So what happens differently in infant baptism and in adult baptism? Dr. Cullman asserted that infant baptism is "a divine act of grace independent of the baby." It is God's gift in which the baby is a passive recipient. "At Golgotha, the prevenient grace of God in Christ is apportioned to all humanity, and entry into Christ's kingdom is opened to them." [145] As an old hymn put it, "tis done, the great transaction's done." This is what Wesley called *gracia praeveniens*. In English it is "prevenient grace" or "previous grace." [146] Prevenient grace is intimated in Romans 5:8-10 {NIV}: "God demonstrates his own love for us in this: "While we were still sinners, Christ died for us." Since we have now been justified, how much more shall we be saved through him! For if, when we were God's enemies, we were reconciled to him (at Golgotha), how much more, having been reconciled, shall we be saved through his life! Through him we have received reconciliation–"God was in Christ reconciling the world unto himself." (2 Corinthians 5:19 {NIV}) In this we are passive; God is the initiating soul force. "Baptism," Dr. Cullman wrote, "is a divine act independent of man's action, an action by which the sacrament, conferred in the Body of Christ,

---

145 Op. Cit., Cullman, 33-34.

146 Ibid., 33.

bestows upon the baptized person the grace that he 'be clothed with Christ.'" (Galatians 3:27 {NIV})[147] He concluded that this is what we celebrate when we baptize an infant or child! It is in this sense that we speak of "baptismal regeneration."

Cullman continued, "But 'to remain in this grace' requires a subsequent human response." Wesley would agree because God's love, like human love, can be rejected or accepted. It is not, in Randy Maddox' words, "monergistic" but "synergistic." As youth or adults we are saved "through our faith in God's grace." Cullman adds helpfully, "Faith after baptism is demanded of all baptized persons (including infants); from adults it is demanded also before." [148] This is a helpful distinction between baptism's celebration of prevenient (preparing) grace for infants and small children, while for youth and adults, baptism involves repentance and forgiveness.

Cullman put it this way: "Baptism points to the future (for infants), and demands for a human response in the future." [149] To paraphrase Cullman, he is saying, in effect, For either infant or octogenarian, God's grace comes before faith. In either instance, the spiritual power of the sacrament was God's gift of grace, not the recipient's faith. God is the operative; the person is 'the subject acted upon.'

In many years of teaching New Testament in Europe's most prestigious seminaries, Cullman mastered Hebrew, Greek, and Latin. These languages helped verbalize our Christian doctrines and convinced him:

> "The reception of this act by the persons baptized consists in nothing else than that they are the passive objects of Christ's dealing, ...really set within the Body of Christ by God. He "is baptized," an unambiguously act of God for which the baptized have only a passive role. Whatever the

---

147 Ibid. 39.

148 Ibid. 52.

149 Ibid. 50.

other considerations to which baptism gives rise, they are to be subordinated to this definition and to be explained by it." [150]

St. Paul went into considerable detail to note that the Church has "many parts but one body." (I Corinthians 12:20 {NIV}) He prefaced that with his reminder that we have "many different kinds of gifts but the same Spirit." (I Corinthians 12:4 {NIV}) Both of these references illustrate importantly Paul's point: "For we were all baptized in the one Spirit into one body – whether Jews or Greeks, slave or free– and were all given the one Spirit to drink." (I Corinthians 12:13 {NIV}) He wrote this more memorably in Ephesians 4:5 {NIV}: "There is one body and one Spirit, just as you were called to one hope – one Lord, one faith, one baptism...."

Paul's term, being "buried with Christ" is, in the opinion of most non-Baptist scholars, a reference to our vicariously identifying with Jesus' Cross and the grave. (Colossians 2:12 {NIV}) It is coupled with "raised with him." Elsewhere and more often, Paul used the metaphor "in Christ" to mean that by faith we are with him in his death and burial and in his resurrection. Regeneration begins with God's initiative of redeeming grace in baptism, and continues in Christ's resurrected presence "so we too live a new life." (Romans 6:4b {NIV}) Paul does not mean a physical identity in either instance.

Response-able Grace

The prototype of baptism is the Israelites' crossing of the Red Sea. God did it! Then came the journey to the Promised Land and the required obedience to the Commandments. That is, although God provided the Exodus as "preparing grace," the wilderness meanderings required the responsible response of the Israelites. Christian baptism is a gift of God that initiates a regenerating process, but baptism for infants or new adult converts is not a *fait accompli*. For infants, parents, the church, and the baptized child all respond to what God has done. Even

150 Ibid. 31.

adults who are new Christians must grow in the knowledge and grace of Jesus Christ. Life happens and baptism is not static; to be spiritually vital, we must grow in grace. Following baptism, for infants or adults, we confirm God's grace in our lives as we "walk with Him along life's pilgrim journey." Following where the Spirit leads us, we can witness with Mary Magdalene, as C. Austin Miles explained, "He walks with me and he talks with me and he tells me I am his own. And the joy we share as we tarry there, none other has ever known."

For children, baptism is the starting point of something that happens. It is more than parental dedication and more than a symbol. Again let us turn to Cullman who believed that in baptism we are made the object of the salvation that Jesus effected on the cross, and our experience of that begins with the covenant of parents and congregation to tell us "Jesus loves us." The "real Presence" of infant baptism is passive on the part of the child; the initiative is God's prevenient grace. The completion of baptismal regeneration is the church's challenge to receive God's saving love and redeeming grace as we gradually understand God's love and make choices accordingly. Cullman was convinced that "in the weekly gatherings of the congregation, the child is placed under special protection against temptations, and in the celebration of Holy Communion, s/he experiences repeatedly the presence of Christ. We, in effect, say as the child grows, 'God loves you and we celebrated that love in baptism; now you prove it to be true with your response!'" [151]

Cullman quotes B. L. Manning whose words are well said:

"Baptism is not dedication. The main thing is not what parents and church will do, though this is important. The main thing is what God has done. It is a sign that Christ claims us all as his own and that He has provided for our redemption to a new way of life when he died on the cross. This is why we baptize children.... We do not baptize them to make them children of God but to celebrate that they are

---

151 Ibid., 49.

already God's. The water of baptism declares that they are already entitled to all God's mercies through the passion of Christ." [152]

For the children of Christian parentage and church nurture, as a child reaches the age of moral accountability, s/he "takes on Christ." With either nurturing love or perhaps a "God moment" in another setting or alone, the child of prevenient grace reciprocates God's love by free will. This is the occasion upon which we can say appropriately, "We are saved by our faith in God's grace." We often call this "accepting Jesus Christ as one's personal savior" or "being saved." Wesley called this "experiential grace." Wesley also used the term, "grace upon grace." We very much need to interpret Confirmation in this way – grace at baptism as preveniently initiated by God and implanted by the Holy Spirit, and confirmed/converting grace in which the youth or adult is the "co-operant." Dr. Randy Maddox' book by the title *Responsible Grace* explains this synchronism so well.

Another dimension of baptismal regeneration is that Paul wrote that children of believers are holy just as the unbelieving spouse is sanctified through the Christian spouse's belief (I Corinthians 7:14 {NIV}). If an infant's parents are "in Christ," and if the congregation takes responsibility for inculcating faith in the baptized child; then the newborn is, according to Paul, "made holy" vicariously. Again, John Wesley called this "prevenient" or "preparing grace." This means that the efficacy or "spiritual power" of what is called too ecclesiastically "baptismal regeneration" is really the Latin term used by Cullman and Wesley–"gracia praeveniens" (prevenient grace).

Cullman sees at least some similarity between baptism into one's faith community and citizenship into a nation. Every baby born into a country has citizenship conferred on him or her without vows of loyalty, heartfelt patriotism, or civic duty, but simply upon being born within geographic national

---

152 Manning. B. L. *Why Not Abandon the Church?*, London: Independent Press, 47.

boundaries. Adults not born in a country must go through the required processes to become "naturalized citizens." However, to enjoy the full dimensions of citizenship like the right to vote, serve on a jury, or serve in the military, a citizen must attain a certain age and level of maturity. So it is that children of Christian parents become members of that faith community upon baptism. The sacrament is a sign-act of God's universal grace. However, the full ramifications of that baptism come only with growth in wisdom, in years, and in "following the commandments of God and walking from henceforth in His holy ways."

Cullman says with regret, "If growth in grace does not follow baptism for the infant or the adult, the sacrament is compromised, disdained, and dishonored, and its fruits destroyed." [153] However, the good news is that you may give up on God by backsliding, but God never gives up on you anymore than the waiting father gave up on the "prodigal son" in Jesus' parable.

John Wesley and United Methodism "on Baptism"

As an Anglican, John Wesley was in a state church. From the time of Constantine in the fourth century, the Protestant state churches in Europe, Scandinavia, and Britain kept the practice of the Roman Catholic Church, a practice that Robert Paul refers to in Germany as "Volkeskirche." Both Europe and Britain were "culturally Christian." Baptism was often called "Christening," a term that meant to be "en Christ-ed" into the Christian family. As natural birth had given a family or "last name," Christening gave the child a "Christian name." These state churches asked every parish to record every birth, including the Christian name given on the day of baptism. Robert Paul calls this the "Volkskirche principle" of a state church, a social paradigm that no longer applies in a secularized society nor by law in free church societies.[154]

In John Wesley's day, almost all children in England, like in Germany, were baptized at birth, given their Christian name,

---

153 Op. Coit., Cullman, 33.

154 Op. Cit., Paul 342.

and recorded in the parish book of records. Also, we must be reminded, Methodism in England was never a Church during Wesley's lifetime. The upshot was that baptism was never emphasized for the Methodist movement in the Church of England. However, Randy Maddox points out, "Wesley's diaries reveal that he also regularly baptized both adults and infants through his ministry." [155]

As for the theology of Baptism, scholars do not agree regarding Wesley's view. We must confess that he remained ambiguous. While he published an abridged edition of his Anglican father's "A Treatise on Baptism," he did not reprint it after 1770. On the other hand, John Wesley also published a tract, "Thoughts on Infant Baptism" in 1751 and reprinted it again and again, as late as 1791. Some competent scholars cited by Maddox argue that Wesley adopted gradually the Puritan theology – that "infant baptism adopts a child into God's covenant of salvation and admission into the Church, believing that regeneration would come later when (and if) the person responsively appropriates this covenant relationship with God." [156] Maddox cites another position: "A few brave souls have suggested that Wesley's comments on baptism reveal an intentional creative tension between sacramentalism and evangelicalism."

Wesley's "way out" of the theological dilemma was to enunciate a dimension of God's initiating grace that comes with birth and is celebrated with infant baptism. "Prevenient grace" of which we have already written, places the sign-act of infant baptism solely in the province of God. Therefore, we are celebrating God's claim of love, or "preparing grace," not the faith of the infant. This doctrine calls upon the parents and the congregation to say, "Just as your family claimed you at birth as a member of your biological family; so in baptism we celebrate God's claim of love upon you." (When a child is born, we give it our family name simply because we love that child. Most married women proudly retain their "birth family name"

---

155 Op. Cit., Maddox, Randy, *Responsible Grace*, 221-223.

156 Ibid., 224.

as a middle name. When that ("in Christ") name is given, we have no idea whether the baby will bring honor or disgrace to the family; we give the name because the child is welcomed and loved before s/he has a "track record." In infant baptism, we give the child its "Christian name" to signify that "Jesus loves all the children of the world."

God's claim on us is like parental claim on a child at birth. At birth God has set his mark and seal on each little child. When Wesley sent his recommended Sunday Service for the American Methodists to use, he deleted the Anglican affirmations of baptismal regeneration as an act of faith, but did not delete that dimension of baptism that, as God's prevenient grace, precedes baptism! The *United Methodist Book of Worship* has a theologically perfect song written by Stanley Farr in 1981 that I had the choir to sing as parents brought their children forward for baptism:

> *"(_____), God claims you, God helps you, protects you, and loves you too.*
>
> *We your family love you so, we vow to help your faith to grow.*
>
> *We are here to say this day that we will help you on your way.*
>
> *And if you should tire or cry, then we will sing this lullaby*
>
> *God claims you, God helps you, protects you, and loves you too."*

In the eighteenth century, Joseph Addison describes what happens when an infant is baptized:

> *"Unnumbered comforts to my soul Thy tender care bestowed before my infant heart conceived from whom those comforts flowed."*

As Emerson Colaw, a prominent Methodist bishop, wrote in 1972, "God's mighty redemptive work in Jesus Christ has already been done. Saying, 'He died for all' does not leave out the children of whom Jesus said, "Let the children come to me...for such is the kingdom of God." We celebrate that universal grace in infant or child baptism, but infant baptism does not pre-empt the subsequent need of the child to accept God's claim upon maturity.[157] Saving grace is co-operant; that is, it requires our response to God's love, and that can come only with maturation.

Obviously, and in contradiction of the language often used by pastors in baptism since 1996, this theology stops short of saying, "This day you became a Christian." We are God's child, but we do not know it cognitively upon being baptized as an infant or very small child. Dr. Randy Maddox has taught us well that Arminianism does not see God's grace as monergistic, but synergistic. Being "in Christ" is a dimension of Methodism's grace theology that comes with the more mature capacity to accept God's saving grace. This is the co-operant dimension. In youth or adults, God's grace can be resisted or accepted. If accepted, then the love of God in infant baptism is confirmed and renewed as a second sign-act of grace – saving grace.

Does this sound complicated? Emerson Colaw helped us here:

"A sacrament is a dramatic reminder that God has done something; it is a symbol of his creative, redemptive power on our behalf.

Finally, though, in traditional United Methodist understanding, the effectiveness of a sacrament depends upon our doing something for its fulfillment." [158]

God's grace is present and operative when a baby is baptized. Wesley called it "preparing grace" or "pre-venient grace," but some role must be retained for human response. Albert Outler and Randy Maddox later called it the "co-operant" role of grace – the person's response. We call it our faith in God's grace. Generally, we associate this with confirmation at about the age

---

157 Colaw, Emerson, *Beliefs of a United Methodist Christian,* Tidings, 1972, 49.

158 Ibid. 84.

of puberty. In his typical conciliatory way, Randy Maddox wrote, "On balance then, it seems best to say that Wesley remained convinced that infant baptism conveyed the regenerating Presence of the Holy Spirit, though he emphasized that the full effectiveness of this gracious Presence emerged gradually, as the developing child responsibly appropriates it." [159] God "nudges." We say, "Yes," "No," or "Wait."

United Methodist Position on Baptism since 1972

Unfortunately, United Methodists are not as well versed in the theology or mode of baptism today as we were in older generations. Therefore, I have chosen to include a chapter on the theology of baptism. Every United Methodist needs to know and be able to articulate what we believe happens when a child, youth, or adult is baptized! Therefore, let us follow the advice of the prophet Isaiah and "Come now, let us reason together" (Isaiah 1:18 {NIV}). The United Methodist Church became official in 1968. The reformulation of its position on baptism began in 1972 and was officially adopted at the General Conference of 1996. Let us trace that development.

Dr. Russell Richey of Duke is probably the eminent historian of American Methodism. His monumental two volumes, *The Methodist Experience in America,* includes a brief history of baptism in American Methodism. Richey writes in retrospect, "Neither the Methodists nor the EUBs brought a highly developed baptismal theology into union. Indeed, both churches were conflicted about the meaning and practice of baptism." [160] Consequently, the young United Methodist Church appointed in 1972 "The Baptism Study Commission." They began the development of a new theology of baptism for United Methodism. Dr. Richey cites four sources beneath the current theological position of The United Methodist Church:

---

159 Op. Cit., Maddox, 225.

160 Richey, Russell, Rowe, Kenneth, Schmidt, Jean, *The Methodist Experience in America,* Vol. I, Abingdon, 2010, 547.

1. The Treatise on Baptism

The *Treatise on Baptism* that John Wesley abridged in 1758 came from his own father's earlier work. Samuel Wesley was an Anglican and believed that baptism was the occasion of being saved from sin and hell.

As Albert Outler wrote, "The young Wesley had grown up in the conventional Anglican soteriology that the basic remedy for original sin was the sacrament of baptism." [161] Indeed, this language from Anglicanism was kept intact in the Methodist Article of Religion XVII: "Baptism...is... a sign of regeneration or the new birth." [162]

Historically, the Articles of Religion were written into the Methodist Episcopal Church constitution in 1808 and cannot be amended, but they have not been followed with any measure of literalism. (They constitute UMC "orthodoxy" but not "orthopraxy." That is, Wesley did not change the Anglican Article, but his sermons did!)

Dr. Richey noted that John Wesley "never thematized theologically between baptismal regeneration in infants and the subsequent necessity for spiritual rebirth." [163] I think Wesley did "thematize theologically" in his 1760 sermon, "The New Birth," when he preached, "Baptism is not the new birth; baptism, the sign, is distinct from regeneration, the thing signified." [164]

However, he "walked that back" in the same sermon: "I do not speak now with regard to infants; it is certain, our Church supposes, that all who are baptized in their infancy are at the same time born again." [165] Granted that Wesley for years seemed to accept his father's traditionally Anglican treatment of infant baptism. However, in Wesley's sermon, "The New Birth," he

---

161 Op. Cit. Wesley, John, *"The New Birth,"* Outler, JWW, Vol. 2, 186.

162 Olson, Harriett, ed., *The Book of Discipline of the United Methodist Church* 2000, ¶103, 63.

163 Op. Cit, Richey, et.al., Vol. I, 547.

164 Op. Cit. Wesley, *"The New Birth,"* Outler, JWW, Vol. 2, 196.

165 Ibid., 197.

could not have been more clear that he had moved to a theological position that could not be called "baptismal regeneration":

"The question is not what was (sic) made in your baptism (do not evade), but what you are now.....Say not then in your heart, 'I was once baptized; therefore I am now a child of God.' Alas, that consequence will by no means hold. How many baptized gluttons and drunkards, baptized liars and common swearers, baptized railers and evil-speakers, baptized whoremongers, thieves, extortioners! What think you? Are these now the children of God? To say that there is no new birth except in baptism is to seal you all under damnation.....You will say, 'But we were washed, we were born again of water and of the Spirit.' So were they....Lean no more on that broken reed, that ye were born again in baptism. No one denies that you were made 'children of God and heirs of the Kingdom'; but notwithstanding this, you are now children of the devil; therefore you must be born again." [166]

Wesley's doctrine of baptism exemplifies the contrast between a systematic theology, which he never wrote, and sixty years of preaching sermons that are not cross referenced.

2. The Consultation on Christian Union

The "Consultation on Christian Union" (COCU) was a great effort in the late twentieth century to merge several denominations of the old "Protestant Establishment." Therefore, regarding baptism, the 1972 UMC document reflected the theology of the Episcopal Church, Lutheran churches, Presbyterian USA, and United Church of Christ. As a consequence, *A Service of Baptism, Confirmation, and Renewal,* was published that used considerable ecumenical theology and language. The new liturgy was officially adopted in 1984. This was a tacit affirmation of "baptismal regeneration," a doctrine prevalent in Angli-

---

166 Wesley, Sermon: *"The Marks of the New Birth,"* JWW, Vol.1, 429.

canism in Wesley's day, but never previously reflected in the Methodist or EUB Book of Discipline prior to 1972.

3. Confirmation Explained

Following the ecumenical position, confirmation was explained, not as conversion nor the initial occasion of regeneration, but as the reaffirmation of the regeneration that occurred at infant baptism. This interpretation was new to historical Methodism and historic Evangelical United Brethren doctrine, but it quickly became the "politically correct" paradigm. (Confirmation did not begin as an almost universal practice until 1968.)

4. Writing of Gayle Carlton Felton

The fourth moving force behind a radically new theology of infant baptism was the prolific writings by one clergyperson. The leadership, note-taking of sessions, subsequent writings, and eventually definitive book by Gayle Carlton Felton of North Carolina became the "voice" of United Methodism. Dr. Felton's work and wording was quoted "everywhere," including in books by Bishop Scott Jones and Bishop Ken Carder.

The influence of theologians and Board of Discipleship staff showed up early. Indeed, as early as 1989 with the publication of a new *United Methodist Hymnal*, the baptismal liturgy for "Children and Those Unable to Answer for Themselves," opens with this statement from the pastor:

> *"Brothers and sisters in Christ, through the sacrament of Baptism, ...we are incorporated into God's mighty acts of salvation and given new birth through water and the Spirit."* [167]

The language of baptismal regeneration was in the new Book of Worship, adopted by the General Conference of 1992. I

---

167 Young, Carlton, ed., *The United Methodist Hymnal*, The Methodist Publishing House, 1989, 39.

149

was chair of the sub-committee that presented it to the plenary session.

In 1996, after eight years of study and editing, Felton's book, *By Water and the Spirit: A United Methodist Understanding of Baptism* was adopted overwhelmingly by the General Conference as the definitive positive of The United Methodist Church. Subsequently, it was quoted by highly respected authors like Bishop Scott Jones and Bishop Kenneth Carder. It quickly became the "textbook" on baptism in all UMC seminaries, and is the theological benchmark in annual conference Boards of Ordained Ministry as they examine candidates for ordination. With that book and that action, baptismal regeneration became the official denominational position.

The "church world" has changed dramatically since the days when nine denominations were named by sociologist Max Weber as "the Protestant Establishment" in America. In more recent years, with secularization of society and the phenomenal growth of Baptist or independent churches, less and less children and grandchildren of Methodist heritage are being baptized. Many Methodist millennials are moving to independent churches where the pastor defines his own doctrines. In lieu of baptism, some churches "dedicate" babies, but do not baptize them. Since United Methodist pastors, like me, have done so little teaching about baptism, many who were "rocked in Methodist cradles" say casually, "All that matters is to love Jesus" and submit to re-baptism by immersion and the dedication of their babies!

What is happening in America in the twenty-first century has at least some similarity to what happened in the early days of Methodism. There has been no more accurate and influential scholar of Wesley's works than Albert Outler of SMU who edited the monumental *Works of John Wesley*. Outler wrote in his own introduction to Sermon # 45 "The New Birth":

"As the tensions in the revival mounted between the claims of the evangelicals regarding conversion, the whole

problem of regeneration in relation both to baptism and justification became more and more urgent." [168]

Outler noted, "It is undeniable that the doctrine of infant baptism as an objective divine action has never had more than a tenuous place in the Methodist tradition." [169] Until the late twentieth century, this has been definitely true of Methodism in America. Today it is true of most independent churches.

Confirmation, Re-baptism, Baptismal Renewal, and Reciprocity in Recognition of Baptism

If we were baptized as an infant celebrating God's love, or even if we are in a church where baptism celebrates only the believer's faith, we will need some mentoring about the sacrament of baptism. Sadly, some churches where infants are not baptized will baptize very young children who, like most children reared in a church, say that they want to give their life to Jesus. They love Jesus in their hearts, but it is a bit disingenuous to say that these children are true believers. Churches who do baptize infants usually wait until about age twelve, to confirm. Then vows professing personal faith are taken by the youth upon his or her reaching an age of moral/ ethical accountability in making choices.

Between baptism and confirmation, parents should keep the vow they took before the congregation: "Will you nurture this child in Christ's holy church, that by your teaching and example s/he may be guided to accept God's grace for her/him self, to profess her/his faith openly, and to lead a Christian life?"

My present pastor follows that long question with a short one, "Will you?"

Far too often, parents depended on Sunday School teachers to carry on the role of Christian nurture between baptism and

---

168 Op. Cit., Outler, Vol. 2, JWW 186.

169 Op. Cit. Outler, Vol. 1, JWW 416.

confirmation. With the precipitous decline in Sunday School attendance, the day probably has come for us to look again at the necessity for the parents to teach the catechism. No pastor can make up with a confirmation class the entire years of childhood when parents should be "training up a child in the way one should go." (Proverbs 22:6 {NIV})

We must take care not to rob a youth of the monumental and memorable "God moment" when one gives one's life to Jesus as Savior from our sins, and subsequent Lord of our decisions and life path. For that reason, Confirmation is "Part II" of a two-part "sign-act" that begins with infant baptism. Confirmation should be more than a "class of twelve year olds."

Confirmation is deeply personal. It is the young person's or the adult's confirming with her or his own free will what the parents did at baptism when God's divinely initiated love, mercy, and grace were celebrated. Confirmation is more than an intellectual assent to a crash course in Bible, church history, and the vows. It is accepting Jesus Christ as the Savior from our sins and embracing him as the Lord of our decisions, life style, morals, and ethics.

Never say, "I was not baptized; I was sprinkled." If you were sprinkled, you were baptized by the mode of sprinkling! If someone asks you, "Have you been sprinkled or baptized?" answer, "I was baptized by sprinkling."

Baptismal Renewal

The psychological value of remembering baptismal waters is very important. While baptism is not to be repeated as a sacrament, it can be renewed as a rite. When youth are being confirmed or when adults have a life changing conversion, baptismal renewal has the same spiritual value as baptism itself, but does not negate one's real baptism. Therefore, we United Methodists urge the pastor to have the "Renewal of Baptism" rite to immediately precede Confirmation, a new spiritual experience, a transfer of church membership, and at least annually for the entire congregation.

The psychological value of water is powerful. Enough should be used that the candidate remembers with gratitude the flowing of water over one's head. Sometimes, for baptismal renewal, water is poured from a pitcher to recall the language of Pentecost when Peter quoted from God's words to the prophet Joel: "I will pour out my Spirit upon all people. Your sons and daughters shall prophesy...." (Acts 2:17 {NIV}) The pastor's words are, "Remember your baptism and be thankful." I often followed that sentence with, "Remember your baptism and be faithful, growing in 'grace upon grace.'"

Summary "On Baptism"

By the second century (202 C.E.) the early church had determined that baptism was initiation of the whole family into the faith community, including infants. In the Greco-Roman culture, if the father made a profession of Christian faith, that family became a "Christian family." From that point, it was the responsibility of the parents to teach the children catechistically what God's love meant preveniently at God's initiative. Then came confirmation and church membership.

Today, religion is in a dramatically changing world. We are in a time of religious shifts comparable to the sixteenth century Protestant Reformation and the Second Great Awaking in the US (c. 1800-1850). The influence of independent churches has drastically decimated the influence of the old "Protestant mainline." Like the days of the early church, today's American society will have mostly adults receiving baptism; therefore in more and more situations, adults will request a "believer's baptism." The reality is that even the adults who were baptized as infants will allow their independent pastors to re-baptize them, usually by immersion. The only way to prevent this is for The United Methodist Church to retain and receive more young adults, and, to teach the meaning of the sacrament of baptism as a sacrament that represents God's irrevocable grace.

We hope that this chapter will bring "more light than heat" onto this important dimension of Methodism's grace theology.

Questions for Discussion and Reflection

Was this chapter helpful in increasing your understanding of baptism? Did you find the Scripture references helpful?

Were you baptized as a baby? If so, as you matured, how did your parents or pastor explain the meaning of your baptism? Did they depend on the Sunday School to teach you the stories of the Bible and what it meant to accept Jesus Christ as your personal savior?

If you were baptized as an infant, were you later confirmed? If so, at what age? Were you guided to accept Jesus as your personal savior, repent of your sins, and join the church?

Did you ever hear of the words "prevenient grace?" If so, what is your understanding of that dimension of God's grace which is completely at God's initiative?

Were you taught that after baptism, it is your responsibility to "grow in grace" as the seasons of life change and your spirituality changes?

Discuss this sentence from Oscar Cullman: "At infant baptism, grace is completely at God's initiative. At Confirmation or youth or adult baptism, God's grace is complemented by your faith; prevenient grace becomes saving grace. But, as we shall see, that is not all God has for us! After being saved, we continue to grow in grace. John Newton had it correct: "tis grace that's brought me safe thus far and grace will lead me on" (or "home"). We call that one's lifelong spiritual journey of "perfecting grace."

Have you experienced the rite of "Renewal of Baptism?" If not, consider it either as a small group comes to a closing session or on the first Sunday of a new calendar year, or some other milestone time in your spiritual journey.

"I observed many years ago: 'It is hard to find in the language of men to explain the deep things of God... But perhaps one might say by the "testimony of the Spirit" I mean an impression on the soul..."

"The Witness of the Spirit II" (1767)

"If we are wise, we will continually be crying to God until his Spirit cry in our heart, 'Abba, Father.'"

"The Witness of the Spirit II" (1767)

"I contend that there is in every believer both the testimony of God's Spirit, and the testimony of his own, that he is a child of God. 'The Spirit himself testifies with our spirit that we are God's children. Now if we are children, then we are heirs – heirs of God and co-heirs with Christ....'" (Romans 8:16 {NIV})

"The Witness of the Spirit" (1746)

"It more clearly concerns the Methodists, so called, clearly to understand, explain, and defend this doctrine, because it is one grand part of the testimony which God has given them in searching the Scriptures, confirmed in the experience of his children, that this great evangelical truth has been recovered, which had been for many years well nigh lost and forgotten."

"The Witness of the Spirit II" (1767)

"None who believes the Scripture as the Word of God can doubt the importance of such a truth as this...If we deny it, there is a danger lest our religion degenerate into mere formality... If we allow it, but do not understand what we allow, we are liable to run into all the wildness of enthusiasm."

"The Witness of the Spirit II" (1767)

"And the outward fruits are doing good to all men, doing no evil to any, and walking in the light..."

"The Witness of the Spirit I" (1746)

"Let none ever presume to rest any testimony of the Spirit which is separate from the fruit of it. ...the immediate consequence will be the fruit of the Spirit–love, joy, peace, long-suffering, gentleness, goodness, fidelity, meekness, temperance."

"The Witness of the Spirit II" (1767)

Chapter Eight

God's Spirit Assuring Us
That We Are Forgiven

"Those who are led by the Spirit of God are children of God. ...When we cry, 'Abba,' it is that very Spirit bearing witness with our spirit that we are children of God"
(Paraphrase, Romans 8:14, 15b-16 (NIV))

Every seeker of experiential grace needs to know that Wesley's long and arduous chapter of faithfulness and near-monastic lifestyle did not bring him what his father Samuel called the "greatest proof of Christianity" – the inward witness. After living a Christian life from childhood, he recognized that something was missing from his relationship with God. Many a faithful pastor or layperson who has been to church for many years and lived a life of impeccable character and careful morality, could say with Wesley that "one thing I lack" – the assurance that my sins are forgiven and that "I know the things of God."

John Wesley was born in 1703 in an Anglican rectory. In his *Journal* in 1742, looking back on his childhood, he copied from his mother's letter her theology of baptism and her efforts to teach him "strictly and carefully that you can be saved only by universal obedience." So it was that he wrote in retrospect on August 1, 1742, "I believe, until I was about ten years old, I had not sinned away the 'washing of the Holy Ghost' which was given me in baptism, having been strictly educated and carefully taught that I could only be saved by universal obedience,

157

that is, by keeping all the commandments of God of which I had been so diligently instructed." [170]

Wesley then added in retrospect:

"The next six or seven years were spent at school...I still read the Scriptures and said my prayers, and what I hoped to be saved by 1) not being so bad as other people, 2) having still a kindness for religion, 3) reading the Bible, 4) going to church, and 5) reading several other books of religion. I continued sinning against the little light that I had except for transient fits of what the divines taught me to call 'repentance.' When I was about twenty-two, my father pressed me to enter into holy orders." [171]

That entry in Wesley's *Journal* has so much similarity with each of our journeys. That is why we devote this chapter to what Wesley called "the witness of the Spirit."

Wesley finished Christ Church College of Oxford, was ordained as an Anglican Deacon, and was elected to the faculty of Lincoln College of Oxford March 17, 1726. He received his M.A. degree in 1727 and accepted his father's plea to become parish assistant, serving the little Wroote parish up in the fen country of Lincolnshire. In 1728, he returned to Oxford to be ordained as an Anglican priest.

"The Holy Club"

Since he was officially a faculty member at Lincoln College, the "head of school" summonsed him to return for academic duty. He arrived back at Oxford, November 22, 1729. It was then that what historians have called "The Holy Club" began meeting with four members. It would be two years before the word "Methodists" was applied. (Dr. Richard Heitzenrater insists on avoiding that name and calling the next six years, "The Rise of

---

170 This exact language is copied by John Wesley from a letter his mother wrote him July 24, 1732.

171 Op. Cit., Outler, Vol. 18, JWW, 243.

Oxford Methodism.") [172]

Wesley wrote in his *Journal*:

"In 1730 I began visiting the prisons, assisting the poor and sick in town, and doing what other good I could by my presence, or my little fortune, to the bodies and souls of all men." [173] He wrote that he "omitted no sort of self-denial, and no occasion of doing good; yet after continuing a few years on this course, 'I could not find that all this gave me any comfort, nor any assurance of acceptance with God.'"

Georgia

In 1735 his father died, making his mother virtually homeless, and four months later, General Oglethorpe invited Wesley to be the ship's chaplain en route to the colony of Georgia and the parish priest at Christ Church in Savannah. The German Moravians deeply impressed him at sea when a severe storm hit. Wesley was scared but the Moravian men, women, and children sang hymns! He was impressed!

As a parish priest in Georgia, Wesley wove into his ministry the Anglo-Catholic spiritual journey and discipline that he adopted from the Book of Homilies that dated back to the Protestant era of young King Edward. (1547-1553)

Wesley's experience in Savannah was a time of "fightings and fears within and without!" He worked at a feverish pace but with some idiosyncrasies:

- **baptized** babies by trine (triple) immersion, even in the dead of winter
- **asked** for confession before Communion if you had been absent for some time
- **met** with the Moravians for spiritual counsel

---

172 Opt. Cit., Heitzenrater, *Wesley and the People Called Methodists*, Abingdon, 1995 42.

173 Op. Cit., Outler, Vol. 18, JWW, 245.

- **read** prayers for German, Italian, and French congregations
- **served** as de facto pastor to a group of Portuguese Jews
- **made** abortive forays to Indian tribes to lead them to Christ
- **traveled** south to Frederica to serve as pastor there after his brother Charles left
- **challenged** the breach of ethics by Thomas Causton whose employee was cheating the Moravians at the "company store." (Causton was uncle and guardian of Sophia Hopkey, the young woman with whom Wesley fell in love, only to see her married to another man.)

In his meetings with the Moravians in Savannah, August Spangenberg asked the Anglican priest some probing questions:

1) Does the Spirit of God bear witness with our spirit that you are a child of God?"

2) Have you the witness within yourself?

3) Do you know Jesus Christ?

To the last, Wesley answered, "I know he is the Saviour of the world?

Spangenberg responded, "True, but do you know that he has saved you?" Wesley answered, "He died to save me." The old Moravian had asked piercing questions and Wesley gave general, even vague, replies.[174] In a later meeting, Wesley asked, "What do you mean by conversion?"

Wesley was very honest with himself and knew that he lacked the witness of the Holy Spirit, the assurance of his personal salvation. His theology was in place, but his experience of God's saving grace became increasingly a matter of grave concern to him. No doubt it brought back a memory of

---

174 Collins, Kenneth, *The Cambridge Companion to John Wesley;* Maddox, Randy, Vickers, Jason, eds., , Cambridge University Press, 2010, 46.

his father's death bed testimony, "The inward witness, son, the inward witness; it is the greatest proof of Christianity." It was also the calm, steady confidence that Wesley had witnessed among the Moravians when the ship to Georgia almost sank during a severe storm.

The bottom line is that in Georgia, a number of things happened that convinced John Wesley of his need for an inner peace, an assurance, a confidence of Paul's affirmation in Romans 8:14-17. {NIV}

After leaving Savannah covertly following evensong and walking through swamps, he boarded a ship in Charleston on December 22, 1737, and wrote, "I took my leave of America (though, if it please God, not forever)." Three days later, he wrote in his diary, "On Christmas Eve, we sailed over the Charleston bar and soon lost sight of land." On board, he was soon counseling with a young African woman, convincing her that she had a soul and was equal to him as a child of God. On February 1, 1738, he wrote, "We climbed into a small boat that in half an hour landed us in Deal (England)."

In London, he had to defend his aborted mission to the Georgia Trustees, and his defense was the first edition of his *Journal.* He wrote, "The faith that I want is a sure trust and confidence in God. To be freed from sin is to be freed from doubt." At age thirty-five, John Wesley was still a "seeker." When he preached as a guest that winter and spring, he was told following several sermons that he could not return to the pulpit of that church.

During the winter and spring, both John and Charles Wesley sought the spiritual direction of Peter Bohler, a Moravian who was en route from Germany to the Carolinas with a layover in England. In March, the Wesleys walked the forty-three miles from London to Oxford with Bohler. On that trip he said, "My brother, my brother, that philosophy of yours must be purged away." [175] On May 4, Bohler left for America. The stage was set for Wesley's life to be changed.Op. Cit.,

---

175 Davies, 50.

Aldersgate

Now we come to May 24, 1738. Wesley opened his Greek
New Testament at 5:00 a.m. He was depressed. At evensong at
St. Paul's Cathedral, he listened to the anthem from Psalm 130
{KJV}: "Out of the depths have I cried unto Thee, oh God..."

He quietly left the cathedral and meandered down "Cheap-
side" that was a street filled with the stalls of what we would
call a flea market. He knew that the Moravians were having
what we would call a "Bible study" on a little side street called
"Aldersgate." He did not want to go, but felt constrained to go.
He went in and eventually a layman began reading *Martin
Luther's Introduction to the Book of Romans.*

Though the words are incredibly familiar to the most
casual student of Wesley, let us listen to them in his own words
that he wrote in his diary later that evening:

> "In the evening I went very unwillingly to a society in
> Aldersgate Street, where one was reading Luther's preface
> to the Epistle to the Romans. About a quarter before nine,
> while he was describing the change which God works in
> the heart through faith in Christ, I felt my heart strangely
> warmed. I felt I did trust in Christ, Christ alone, for salva-
> tion, and an assurance was given me that He had taken
> away my sins, even mine, and saved me from the law of sin
> and death." [176]

Some of us are like John Wesley, in that we spent our childhood in a Christian family and a warm, loving local church,
and were confirmed at about age twelve. Like Wesley, we
lived with high standards of morality, ethics, and self-control
of what he called "our tempers." Since our earliest memory,
we have answered in the affirmative if someone asked, "Are
you a Christian?" However, if pressed as Wesley was by the
Moravian in Georgia or by Peter Bohler, we have a lack of
inner peace or, as Wesley and St. Paul called it, "the witness of
the Spirit." Scholars and preachers tend to interpret Wesley's

---

176 Ibid., 51.

experience differently. Once when I heard Rupert Davies, a brilliant British student of Wesley, teach in the New Room in Bristol, he described Aldersgate in words he later wrote in his book, *Methodism:*

"Psychologically, there is no doubt that this was a complete turning point in the life of John Wesley. Until now his immense spiritual and mental energies had been mostly directed upon himself... He had spent most of his life brooding over the state of his soul and how to improve it. Now those energies were released and immediately directed outwardly...

Theologically, May 24, 1738, was no less important... Wesley was as orthodox in his doctrine and "catholic" in his knowledge of the church fathers' writings as any man. For fourteen years, he had followed the path of 'inward and outward holiness' and he had arrived nowhere. He wrote in his Journal upon his return to London from his missionary venture in Georgia, 'What have I learned about myself? That I who went to America to convert others, was never myself converted to God.' [177] Now through Bohler, he saw that he had omitted one vital stage on his way to holiness, in fact, the very entrance to the Way–his personal faith in Jesus Christ, without which it is useless to try to be holy. Faith leading to holiness, not holiness itself, was now his understanding of the Christian life.[178]

John Wesley, on the date in question, was assured that Christ had taken away his sins, even his. This became known as his "doctrine of assurance" that he called "witness of the Spirit." He distinguished for himself and the first century of Methodism the interplay of the "witness of the Holy Spirit" and the witness of our own spirit." [179]

---

177 Ibid., 49.

178 Ibid., 52.

179 Ibid., 53.

Emotions are slippery. I therefore took heart at Wesley's confession that the fruits of the Spirit that Paul listed in Galatians 5:22-23 {NIV} may be "clouded for a while during the time of strong temptation and that our joy may leave us during our lives' hours of trial." But even this is generally restored with increase...[180]

Richard Heitzenrater has corrected the conventional wisdom about Wesley's Aldersgate experience in two ways.

- One is that within months, Wesley was writing in his diary that while he still had the peace of being forgiven, he did not have the joy of his first days of experiential grace.

- Secondly, contrary to most preachers who often tell of their experiences similar to Aldersgate, Wesley very seldom repeated the words he wrote in his diary on the night of May 24, 1738.

Perhaps you will appreciate why Wesley did not regale his congregations about Aldersgate. One clue is seen in the language he used to describe the experience–"strangely warmed." To appreciate this, we need to know about John Wesley's own disposition! He was not a man who based his faith on human enthusiasm. He felt awkward describing his feeling as "joy." The feeling at the Aldersgate meeting was therefore recorded as "strangely warmed." It makes some of us take heart to read:

"There may be foretastes of joy, peace, and love – and those not delusive, but really from God – long before we have the witness in ourselves, before the Spirit of God witnesses with our spirits that we have forgiveness of sins. But it is by no means advisable to rest here. Continue crying to God until his Spirit cry in our heart, 'Abba, Father.' This is the privilege of all children of God." [181]

---

180 Op. Cit., Wesley, John, Sermon: *"Witness of the Spirit II,"* JWW, Vol. 1 298.

181 Ibid., 298.

As he processed in his mind what he would later call "experimental divinity," he came to describe the witness of the Holy Spirit as "trust and confidence." We know the distinction of "trust" from "passion" in our experience of marital love. Even Martin Luther said, "I am not passionately in love with Kathryn every day, but I trust our love because of my confidence in her character and her love for me."

John the Elder wrote, "We love because God first loved us." (I John 4:19 {NIV}) John is clearly not placing the witness of the spirit on our emotions, but on God's love that was demonstrated through Jesus.

Witness is not sheer emotionalism. A witness is someone who testifies to what he or she saw or heard. "Bearing witness" is simply telling the truth and might not carry any emotional feeling with it. In "witness of the Spirit," God is confirming in a "language of the soul." John Wesley was a consecrated man before May 24, 1738. Indeed, he was a holy man, but he was not a happy man. For over three years, he had seen in the German Moravians something he lacked – the quiet confidence of "knowing" one's sins forgiven.

Under the mentoring of Moravian Peter Bohler, Wesley became open to the defining moment in his spiritual journey at Aldersgate Street in London on May 24,1738. He later cited the doctrine of "witness of the Spirit" as a Methodist fundamental by saying:

"It more nearly concerns the Methodists (so called) clearly to understand, explain, and defend this doctrine because it is one grand part of the testimony which God has given them to bear to all mankind. It is by his (God's) peculiar blessing upon them (the Methodists) in searching the Scriptures, confirmed by the experience of his children, that this great evangelical truth has been recovered, which had been for many years well nigh lost and forgotten." [182]

---

182 Ibid., 285-286.

Professor William Abraham's words speak for most inter-preters of Aldersgate: "Wesley had met God for himself." [183] By 1739 he was beginning to integrate all that he had learned and experienced into a new vision of the Christian tradition." [184]

From that, all Methodists take our own cue for our spiritual journey. Our own "Aldersgate" often comes after many years of faithful discipleship. We do not have a "God moment" every day, week, month, or year. However, when we do, we have the "confidence to tell." Jesus' most common invitation was simple and unexplored: "Follow me." His assuring words, at least even-tually, become our experience of assurance, "Whoever comes will in no way be cast out."

Wesley's Two Essays, "Witness of the Spirit"

John and Charles Wesley had their critics about the assur-ance of knowing our sins forgiven. In order to both explain and defend his conviction concerning the assurance of one's salva-tion, Wesley wrote and distributed two essays entitled *Witness of the Spirit,* based on Paul's assurances in Romans 8:16 {NIV}: "The Spirit himself testifies with our spirit that we are God's children."

To develop Paul's metaphors for "witness of the Spirit," Wesley used terms like "deep things of God," "hard to find in the language of men," and "the inward impression on the soul." [185] He quoted the book he loved so much, "And this is how we know he lives in us: We know it by the Spirit he gave us." (I John 3:24 {NIV})

Wesley is careful to say, "I do not mean that the Spirit of God testifies this by any outward voice; nor even always by an inward voice. Again Wesley uses commonplace language, saying that God "so works upon the soul by his immediate influence that the stormy wind and troubled waters subside

---

183 Op. Cit, 8.

184 Ibid., 11.

185 Op. Cit, Wesley, Sermon, *"Witness of the Spirit,"* JWW, Vol 1, 274.

and there is a calm. We are clearly satisfied that our iniquities are forgiven and our sins are covered." [186] Referring to Paul's phrase, "spirit of adoption" in Romans 8:15, Randy Maddox insists that "adoption" is the internalizing of Christianity's central goal." [187] He deducts this from Wesley who called it "restoring the due relations between God and humanity by uniting forever the tender Father and the grateful, obedient child." [188] Wesley continued, "After twenty years' farther consideration I see no cause to retract any part of this." [189]

In his two essays "Witness of the Spirit I & II," Wesley used three arguments to defend the doctrine "witness of the Spirit":

1. The scriptural foundation is primary, particularly Paul's words on which the essays are based. Wesley considers this an objective foundation for the "witness of the Spirit" or "blessed assurance":

> "All who are led by the Spirit of God are the children of God. For you did not receive the spirit of fear, but you have received the spirit of adoption. When we cry, 'Abba, Father' it is that very Spirit bearing witness with our spirit that we are children of God, and if children, then heirs, heirs of God and joint heirs with Christ."
>
> **Romans 8:14-17a {NIV}**

2. The philosophical foundation for the doctrine is sheer logic: We cannot really know that God loves us until his Spirit bears witness with our spirit. We cannot love God until we know in our own spirit that God has first loved us. We will not joyfully live "holiness of life and heart" until we have this "witness

---

186 Ibid., 287.

187 Op. Cit., Randy, *Responsible Grace*, 168.

188 Wesley, John, "An Earnest Appeal to Men of Reason and Religion," JWW, Vol. 11, Abingdon, 1989, 55.

189 Ibid., 287.

of the Spirit" that Wesley first experienced on May 24, 1738. Thus, logically, the foundation for our "house of faith" is laid in Romans 8:14-17.

3. The subjective foundation for the "testimony of the Spirit" is, in Wesley's words, "hard to find in the language of men." He sees this witness as one of the "deep things of God."

> "I mean an inward impression of the soul, whereby the Spirit of God immediately and directly witnesses to my spirit that I am a child of God, that 'Jesus Christ hath loved me and given himself for me,' that all my sins are blotted out, and I, even I, am reconciled to God." [190]

Charles Wesley, as was his custom, converted his brother's prose to verse:

> *"How can a sinner know his sins on earth forgiven?*
>
> *How can my gracious Savior show my name inscribed in heaven?*
>
> *What we have felt and seen with confidence we tell,*
>
> *And publish to the ends of earth the signs infallible!*
>
> *We by his Spirit prove and know the things of God,*
>
> *The things which freely of his love he hath on us bestowed.*
>
> *Our nature's turned, our mind transformed in all its powers,*
>
> *And both the witnesses are joined – The Spirit of God with ours."*

Psychological issues with "knowing our sins forgiven"

Allow me a personal word about "witness of the Spirit." I grew up in a very evangelistic church environment where the preacher gave an altar call and promised that we would have our own Aldersgate experience. Many times, at my local

---

190 Op. Cit., Wesley, John, Sermon: "Witness of the Spirit, II", JWW, Vol 1, 287.

church's annual revival and at four years' ten-day attendance at a "holiness Methodist camp meeting," I went forward in good faith and with high expectations of feeling my heart "strangely warmed." Clergy and laity would gather around us, lay hands on us, and try to "pray us through." Others would get up, some crying, some shouting, some in silence. I was repeatedly determined to wait for some "feeling." It never came.

When I was sixteen, the camp meeting altar call was for those willing to give God our life "in full -time Christian service." I went forward. The preacher wisely had the four of us who had gone to the altar to sign our names to a paper stating our commitment of our professional life to God. That was July. On January 3, my signed letter came in the mail. I kept my vow but without the feeling that I so desperately prayed for.

In my senior year of college, I was appointed as pastor of a church. After seminary when I served a four-point rural circuit, a large church pastor asked me to be the "minister of the week" for his youth. One morning, he came up to the Blue Ridge Mountains camp to lead our devotions.

I was a theological Fundamentalist who did not really know God as my heavenly Father who loved me. I saw him as my judge and Jesus as my Savior and me as a "defender of the faith." That morning, the pastor read from John 15 {NIV}. He first read verses 14-15:

"You are my friends I no longer call you servants because a servant does not know his master's business. I have called you my friends because everything that I learned from my Father, I have made known to you."

Then he closed by reading John 15:11: "I have told you this so that my joy may be in you and that your joy may be complete." When chapel was over I confessed to him that I did know this "witness of the Spirit" that John Wesley described as his experience at Aldersgate. We sat down on a rock overlooking a vast mountain gorge with a majestic mountain in the distance.

It was that morning, in that setting, that I came to believe my own "Aldersgate." Considering my emotional make-up, I might never have a feeling of being "strangely warmed." Friends develop a trust and confidence, not necessarily based on emotional feelings. Instead of the feeling that I wanted so much, I trusted in God's love and developed a confidence of being saved through faith in God's redeeming grace and by the authority of the Scriptures. God is my Father and I am God's adopted child, just as Paul said in Romans 8!

Your experience of the witness of the Spirit might be a wave of peace, a deep sense of release from guilt, or an eviscerating yell of "YES!" Or, the witness of the Spirit for you might be more like mine – a sense of trust in God's love more than in my feelings, a confidence in God's grace more than in my believing faith.

Whatever the dynamics of your "God-moment," "witness of the Spirit" is a Methodist fundamental!

Questions for Discussion and Reflection

This chapter has presented as accurately as we know one of the major emphases of Wesley and the first century of Methodism. How important do you feel this assurance of God's love and forgiveness is to being a Christian?

God's loving presence will find you where you are and as you are. If you do not yet have this "blessed assurance," do you seek it? Do you think you are seeking an experience like someone else described from their journey? Are Christians like products of a cookie cutter or like snowflakes? Do you have some foreboding sense of being less of a Christian because you do not have "feeling?"

Was this chapter helpful? What have you read in this chapter that gives you pause? With what do you disagree?

After reading and discussing this chapter, what do you see as your next step in your own spiritual journey?

Wesley insisted that the Spirit of God does not cease working in us after we have first experienced God's saving grace. He used the term often, "grace upon grace."

"There is scarce any word in Holy Writ which has given more offense than this–Christian perfection. The word 'perfect' is what many cannot bear. The very sound is an abomination to them. Hence some have advised to lay aside the use of such expression. But are they not found in the oracles of God. Whatever God hath spoke; that we will preach."

Christian Perfection (1741) (paraphrase)

"By salvation I mean not barely, according to the vulgar notion, 'deliverance from hell, or going to heaven,' but a present deliverance from sin, a restoration of the soul to its primitive health, its original purity, a recovery of the divine nature; the renewal of our souls after the image of God, in righteousness and true holiness, in justice, mercy, and truth."

John Wesley

"Everyone who lives on milk being still an infant, is unskilled in the word of righteousness. Solid food is for the mature, for those whose faculties have been trained to distinguish good from evil. Therefore let us go on to perfection"

Hebrews 6:1 {NIV}

"Ask and you will receive, and your joy will be complete."

John 16:24b {NIV}

"Reformation thought does not take seriously enough the possibility of holiness in Christian living."

John Baille, Scot Presbyterian

Chapter Nine

Perfecting Grace:
Grace Upon Grace

Though "grace is grace" and we don't want to slice and dice it, you have now read a chapter describing "preparing" or "prevenient grace" and a chapter dedicated to "saving" or "justifying" grace. I included a chapter on baptism. The third dimension was once called "sanctification," and Wesley called it "Christian Perfection," but the term preferred today is "perfecting grace." Adding the "ing" indicates a gradual growth in grace. Becoming a new Christian does not only fail to tame our demons; they are not even named! The word "disciple" means "learner"; therefore, we believe in "grace upon grace." We turn in this chapter to the potential of perfecting grace.

"The Peculiar Doctrine Celebrated to our Trust"

Fifteen months after his life changing religious experience at Aldersgate in 1738, Wesley was writing about the need to experience "grace upon grace." So, what is this dimension of grace for the ordinary Christian? Wesley wrote, "They speak of sanctification (or holiness) as if it consisted chiefly, if not wholly, in these two points: 1) doing no harm and 2) doing good...and helping our neighbor. I believe it to be an inward thing, namely, 'the life of God in the soul of man,' a 'participation of the divine nature,' 'the mind that was in Christ,' or, 'the renewal of our heart, after the image of Him that created us.'" [191] For this insight, Wesley cites Philippians 2:5, "Let the

---

191 Wesley, John, *Journal 3*, JWW, Vol. 19, 97.

mind be in you that was in Christ Jesus," and Colossians 3:10, "...having clothed yourselves with the new self, which is being renewed in knowledge according to the image of its creator." (Wesley's translation)

Wesley was convinced that, "for the sake of propagating this truth, He appeared to have raised us up." [192] He also called it, "This peculiar doctrine celebrated to our trust." Yet, the doctrine caused so much misunderstanding, misquoting of scripture, and misquoting of Wesley that he asked publicly at the 1768 conference, "I ask, once and for all, 'Shall we defend this perfection or give it up?'" [193]

They did not give it up!

Less than a year before his death at age eighty-eight, Wesley was still writing about perfecting grace. Perfecting grace cannot be omitted as a Methodist fundamental because historically and experientially, our walk with the Lord does not end with "being saved." Colin Williams of Australian Methodism speaks for the majority of serious Wesley scholars: "There can be no doubt of the importance of the doctrine of perfection in the history of Methodism." [194] Wesley considered his doctrine of Christian perfection the "grand depositum" of Methodism." [195]

Bishop Nolan B. Harmon wrote in his classic, *Understanding The Methodist Church:*

" The doctrine of Christian perfection has been the one specific contribution which Methodism has made to the Church universal. In this one doctrine we stand by ourselves and utter a teaching that reaches up fearlessly and touches the very scepter of God's grace. If we can live

---

192 Op. Cit., Telford, Vol. VIII, 238.

193 Op. Cit., Heitzenrater, 242.

194 Op. Cit., Williams, 167.

195 Op. Cit., Telford, 238.

one day without sin, we can live two, then many. Why not all?" [196]

Bishop Scott Jones gave a similar commentary:

"As the power of sin decreases, one's behaviors improve and inward sin diminishes as well." [197]

The terms "Christian Perfection," "Perfect Love," and "sanctification" sound sanctimonious and "over the top" for many Christians. Wesley did not believe that instantaneous sanctification can be documented by Holy Scripture. He used the term "inward tempers" by which, in today's parlance he meant what Randy Maddox calls, "an enduring or habitual disposition of a person." [198]

Perhaps it will be helpful for me to recall how perfecting grace first became a part of my grace theology. When I was a teenager, a wise minister went to the blackboard and wrote on it some of the sins we might have committed. Then he said, "When you were saved, these sins were erased," and he wiped the board clean. Then he said, "Now the rest of your life will not be like this blank blackboard; something will be written on it. If you stop with your new birth in Christ, you might well simply write more sins of thoughts, words, or acts. However, if you are led by the Holy Spirit, if you trust and obey the Lord, you will write a new script."

Then he hung up a banner on which was printed the words of Romans 12:2 {Phillips}, "Do not let the world around you squeeze you into its own mold, but let God re-mold your minds from within; so that you may prove in practice that the Plan of God for you is good, meets all His demands and moves you

---

196 Harmon, Nolan B., *Understanding the Methodist Church*, Abingdon, 1961, 70.

197 Op. Cit., Jones, Scott, 199.

198 Op. Cit., Maddox, 198.

toward the goal of true maturity." [199] I am nearly eighty-three as I write these words in the year of our Lord, two thousand and eighteen, but I have never forgotten the impact of that lesson in the meaning of perfecting grace. Romans 12 is the roadmap to a life of perfecting grace.

Long ago I highlighted in several of my Bibles and attached to Romans 12 a word from Paul to his favorite church – the church at Philippi, Greece:

"I am not saying that I 'have it altogether, that I have it made. But I am well on my way, reaching out for Christ who has so wondrously reached out for me. Friends, don't get me wrong; I'm not saying I am an expert in all of these, but I've got my eye on the goalposts to which God is beckoning me on. I'm off and running and I'm not turning back."

Philippians 3:12-14 {The Message}

This paradigm is somewhat reflected in the doggerel I have seen in Christian ladies' kitchens, "Don't criticize me; God ain't done with me yet."

Wesley wrote in his sermon, "Christian Perfection," "No one can say, 'I have not sinned,' but God is ready and willing both to forgive our sins and to save us from them in the future." When we commit ourselves to a "grace-growth" toward perfection, God "installs a pacemaker" that "tunes" our heart so that we are henceforth "in tune with the Infinite." The Holy Spirit nudges our thoughts, words, and deeds so that our hearts are in sync with God's will. In Colin Williams' words, "The perfect Christian is holy, not because he has risen to a required moral standard, but because he lives in a state of unbroken fellowship with Christ." [200]

Harry Denman once taught my family at our parsonage breakfast table how he prayed the Lord's Prayer every morning,

---

199 Phillips, J. B., *Letters to the Young Churches*, Macmillan, 1956, 28.

200 Op.Cit., Williams, 175.

"Thy will be done – in me, in me – on earth as it is in heaven."

To this saintly layman, perfection meant a daily, conscious conformity to the will of God as he understood it. This is what Wesley meant when he used the term "perfection of the pilgrim."

A pilgrim is a person progressing toward a goal. This is what we today understand in the idiom, "perfecting grace." William Sangster was one of British Methodism's greatest preachers. He wrote:

> "Perfection is an unfortunate term. It has about it an idea of something that is finished and fixed. That is not what the Christian means. He means that if we can live one day without sin we can live two; if two, then many – why not all? So there is a growing in grace and a drawing closer and closer to God each day." [201]

In a letter to brother Charles, in 1762, John Wesley says:

> "By perfection, I mean the humble, gentle, patient love of God and man ruling all the tempers, words and actions, the whole heart and the whole life. I do not include the impossibility of falling from it and I do not contend for the term 'sinless.' I believe that being perfected in love usually comes many years after justification, but it may be within five years or five months after it." [202]

John Wesley said that orthodoxy was not so important as "ortho-praxy." That is, "practice what you will now be preaching." If you owe a debt, go pay it and your creditor will know you have changed. If you have been a "deadbeat dad," take your children's mother the delinquent child support. If you have been negligent of parents, grandparents, or church attendance, change!! Wesley said that orthodox belief is not as important as life change. As a Christian, we are called to stop bad habits of

---

201 Op. Cit Harmon, 73.

202 Chilcote, Paul; Collins, Kenneth, eds.; Wesley, John, "Arminian Mago zine," 1783, JWW, Vol. 13, 2013, 199.

language and abusive behavior, reconcile estranged relationships, and enjoy new life enhancements.

The process of perfecting grace means changing your lifestyle in demonstrable, observable, empirical ways. Jesus was more literal in the "Sermon on the Mount." He said, "If you are offering your gift at the altar and there remember that your brother has something against you, leave our gift there in front of the altar. First, go and be reconciled to your brother; then come and offer your gift." (Matthew 5:23-24 {NIV}) He said, "If someone forces you to go one mile, go with him two miles." (Matthew 5:41 {NIV}) (Roman officers could coerce a Jew to take their backpacks one mile, but no more.) Those would be specific, observable indications in Jesus' culture that you were a very unusual person!

The Setback of Sanctification by the Holiness Movement

When I was fourteen, someone convinced my mother to send me to John Wesley Holiness Camp Meeting for ten days. There were a hundred youth in the antiphonal choirs. The preachers were spellbinders who told emotionally motivating stories from their ministries, always closing with an altar call. The theology emphasized the need to first be saved from our sins and then to be sanctified. Being sanctified defined "holy living" as abstinence from movies, dancing, kissing, and holding hands! For the girls, it meant no make-up. I never "prayed through" to receive the gift of sanctification. However, I learned the language of that "holiness theology," and I followed much of the "holiness code." I abstained from movies for two years and never learned to dance, but did not abstain from kissing girls and holding their hands!

John Wesley Holiness Camp Meeting was the setting in which God changed my life. The month I was sixteen, in an open tabernacle covered in shavings, the altar call was to come and kneel if you would give your life to God in "full time Christian service." I went and knelt and never reneged. I have had to "unlearn" a lot of the camp meeting theology and move beyond the taboos, but I am indebted to those preachers for being God's way of getting into my life vocationally.

I had no clue at sixteen that when I was nineteen I would be a senior in college and appointed as pastor of a Methodist Church! As my farmer father would have said in one of his idiomatic expressions, "I did not know 'B' from 'bullsfoot." My aunt told me years later that Mama prayed for me when I was born that one day I would be a Methodist preacher.

I only wish that the preachers at the camp meeting had emphasized the peace of perfecting grace rather than the taboos of what they erroneously identified as holiness. I never became sanctified. However, I learned a gospel hymn that has stayed with me even in some of life's rough patches:

"There's within my heart a melody, Jesus whispers sweet and low,

Fear not, I am with thee, peace be still, in all of life's ebb and flow.

Tho' sometimes He leads through waters deep, trials fall across the way;

Tho' sometimes the path seems rough and steep, see his footprints all the way

Jesus...fills my every longing, keeps me singing as I go."

I love that old hymn and many others taught me by the troubadour musicians of the holiness camp meetings. How sad that the holiness movement that meant so sincerely to preserve the doctrine of perfecting grace allowed it to be hijacked by a counter cultural code that was almost cultic. Many of us who were called to preach through that movement had to be vitalized by amazing grace!'

What Wesley Did Not Mean

We must get past what the old holiness movement said about perfecting grace and ask, "What did John Wesley say? He did not mean a puritanical dress code nor did he mean refusing to go to a theater! Wesley wrote:

"I think it was the latter part of the year 1740 that I had a conversation with the Bishop of London at Whitehall. He asked me what I meant by perfection. I told him without disguise or reserve. When I ceased speaking, he said, 'Mr. Wesley, if this be all you mean, publish it to all the world.' I answered, 'My lord, I will.'"

And accordingly, Wesley wrote and published the sermon, "Christian Perfection."

To be fair and accurate, let us first enunciate what Wesley did not mean by Christian perfection:

Christian infallibility. No one possesses absolute knowledge, perfect judgment, consistent performance, or total control of what Wesley called one's "tempers." ("Tempers" in the eighteenth century meant "disposition.") Wesley called that "angelism," and said he wanted a holiness for real people engaged in real life. He wrote in his long tract, "A Plain Account of Christian Perfection," "I believe a person filled with the love of God is still liable to these involuntary transgressions." [203] He said to the conference in Bristol in 1758, "Even the most perfect must pray for themselves, 'forgive us our trespasses.'" [204]

Superiority. Moving deeper into the "mind which was in Christ" must not breed a rank of spiritual superiors. The effect must be humility, not pride. Wesley wrote, "'Sinless perfection' is a term I never use. We cannot avoid thinking wrong. I expect not to be freed from actual mistakes till this mortal puts on immortality."

---

203 Outler, Albert, *John Wesley,* Oxford Press, 1964, 287.

204 Ibid.,, 285.

Immunity from life's infirmities. Being sick, falling victim to natural law disasters, being wounded or killed by war or crime, and losing one's job must not be seen as the lack of Christian perfection. It is not, in Steve Harper's words, "vaccination from reality." [205] Regarding sickness, it is patently not true that "if you have sufficient faith, you will be healed." If faith healed all who are infirm, when the disease finally took them, would it be an indication that their faith had lessened? Even the most devout Christians die to the same degree as everyone else –100 percent.

Instantaneous "faith accompli." One of my teenage memories is hearing people give specific dates for their conversion and their being sanctified. We can certainly have a liberating experience of surrendering to God some habit, relationship, or attitude that has denied the Holy Spirit's empowering us to grow. However, once that block is moved, we must "press on to the high calling which is ours in Christ Jesus." The devil is no slacker. We are constantly being tempted in thought, word, and deed, and we at least occasionally can be seduced by evil in some form.

What Wesley Did Mean

Two nuances of grammar are theologically important. Wesley spoke of "going on" to perfection more than of having arrived. To claim that we have arrived at perfection reflects Pharisaism and sanctimonious spiritual pride.

The second grammatical nuance is "perfecting grace." This is in keeping with Wesley's description of the Christian journey as "grace upon grace." Wesley's problem was how to define a life of perfection for "imperfects" like us! We must not look at humankind through rose-colored glasses, forgetting creaturely limitations on the one hand and the continuing effects of original sin on the other.

"Perfecting grace is," in Bishop Ken Carder's words, "a gift [of God] emerging from friendship with and obedience to

---

205 Op. Cit., Harper, 93.

Christ, a process of maturing in discipleship until the heart is habitually inclined to do what is right. Perfection must never be seen as perfectionism." [206]

Wesley borrowed from a wide and deep stream of piety in his insistence on a goal of "perfect love" and its two-dimensional focus of "loving God and loving neighbor." He says, "This is the sum of Christian perfection: It is all comprised in that one word, LOVE." [207] Robert Cushman insisted that neither the saints of Catholicism, nor Anglicanism, nor Martin Luther, nor John Calvin, nor the Moravians understood perfecting grace as Wesley did. [208] Wesley had found in his own experiences of seeking to be a holy man while in Oxford and Georgia that holiness is not attainable through self-discipline. Perfect love is our responsive embrace of God's gift of the Holy Spirit. It is God's work of grace, not our work of spirituality, nor as Wesley somewhat sarcastically said, "angelism."

There has probably never been a hymnal among Wesleyans that did not include Charles Wesley's classic, "Love Divine, All Love Excelling." As you meditate on its phraseology, Charles gives us a superb definition of perfecting grace:

"Breathe, oh breathe, thy loving spirit into every troubled breast,

Let us all in thee inherit, let us find that second rest.*

Take away our bent to sinning, Alpha and Omega be

End of faith as its beginning, set our hearts at liberty."

*Note: the "first rest" was being saved from our sins; the "second rest" is the inner peace and empowering of the Holy Spirit to "deliver us from evil," personally and societally.

---

206 Op. Cit., Carder, 63.

207 Wesley, Sermon, *"On Perfection,"* JWW, Vol 3, 74.

208 Op. Cit., Cushman, 46.

In another hymn, Charles has us sing,

"O may Thy love possess my whole, my joy, my pleasure, and my crown;

Strange fires far from my heart remove; my every act, word, thought be love!"

In the historical context of Methodist "experimental divinity," what we mean by Christian perfection is this – we grow in grace, we draw "closer to Thee," until, except for constant human frailty and cultural blindness of which we are not conscious, we can live in relational harmony with God.

Wesley often defined perfect love as Jesus' two-fold summary of the law and prophets – love God with heart, mind, soul, and strength, and, love your neighbor as yourself. Is not "growing in the grace and knowledge of Jesus Christ" a goal common to every Christian tradition?

Christian Perfection Across The Years

Beginning about the 1860's sanctification was maligned by its friends and caricatured by its opponents. In 1867 a "Holiness Association" was formed in Chicago that identified Christian perfection with a puritanical lifestyle called "the holiness code." Outler reflects on the negative results of the "taboos" of the holiness code:

"This syndrome of self-righteousness amongst the holiness people led the 'mainstream' to throw out the Wesleyan baby of true holiness with the 'second blessing' bath water." [209]

There was no "perfect love" in either position. Each extreme position castigated the other.

As strident voices prevailed, the most sane and scholarly voice of Methodism was ignored – that of John Miley who was a prominent pastor before, during, and after the Civil War.

---

209 Op. Cit. Outler, *Evangelism and Theology in the Wesleyan Spirit*, 125.

Lacking seminary education, he had taught himself suffi-ciently to be appointed to the position of Chair of Systematic Theology at the new Drew Theological Seminary in 1873. Miley tried to bridge the gap between the radical holiness followers who insisted that sanctification eradicated the root of sin: "Grace penetrates into the texture of our spiritual being, and destroys (sin)." That radical position was called "entire" or "complete sanctification" and would eliminate the possibility of backsliding.

Miley responded that sanctification is not the eradication of sin, but the repression of sinful "affections." He defined perfecting grace in a realistic way that should have become the position of Methodism in the 20th century. Following being saved, Miley called for "a deeper work, a clearer spir-itual discernment, the easier victory over temptation, the greater strength to do one's duty, the intenser love for neigh-bor, and the closer communion to God." [210]

That is an incredibly accurate and deeply needed defini-tion of perfecting grace. Thomas Langford has said, "Miley stood at the collision point of the old and new in Methodist theological interpretation." After him, most Methodist theo-logians moved in a different direction." [211] Mainstream Meth-odism, to its detriment, forsook the very doctrine that Wesley believed God had entrusted uniquely to the Methodists.

Miley was ignored. By the time of the 1894 General Confer-ence, the composite address of the bishops virtually invited those who would "push" holiness to leave. The result was the founding of the Nazarene Church. The Methodist preachers who "preached sanctification and holiness" were for the most part relegated to small membership churches. The loss was great for us all.

The mainstream of Methodism from 1894 onward woefully neglected the essence of Wesley's grand depositum of perfect-

---

210 Miley, John, *Systematic Theology,* Hendrickson Publishers, 1989, 363.

211 Langford, Thomas A. *Practical Divinity,* Abingdon, 1983, 115.

ing grace until its recovery by Albert Outler of Perkins School of Theology at Southern Methodist University in the 1960's. Since that time, there has been distinguished caravans of scholars who have added new life and new scholarship to Wesley's prescient understanding of perfecting grace.

My Journey with Perfecting Grace

This is not an autobiography! However, I hope that you might find yourself in one or more of the seasons of my spiritual journey. I became a rather well-read student of biblical literalism and "the verbal, plenary inspiration of the Bible." I rejected all forms of biblical criticism during all my college years. Then, I had a life changing "God moment."

When I was twenty years old I heard Dr. E. Stanley Jones. He was a graduate of Asbury Theological Seminary who devoted his life to missionary work in India among both the untouchables and the Brahmin – Hindu, Muslim, Sikh, Communists, and Christians. He has been called "the longest tested Christian missionary and evangelist since St. Paul." He was once elected as a Methodist bishop, but immediately resigned. Dr. Martin Luther King credited Jones' biography of Mahatma Gandhi with King's commitment to non-violence as the paradigm of social change to which he would devote his own life. Dr. Jones moved without portfolio on five continents among the statesmen of his time.

Borrowing a Hindu concept which in the Sanskrit means "religious exertion," he created in 1930 the Christian Ashram as an austere and disciplined retreat for enhancing perfecting grace. To me, even as a youth, he was the epitome of a Christlike Christian.

In July, 1955, E. Stanley Jones came to High Point College in North Carolina, and alongside my saintly mother who had read his books and my fiancée, I heard him. First, he taught us to rehearse the first Christian creed as we raised our forefinger and middle finger and affirmed, "JESUS IS LORD."

Later in his sermon/lecture, he stepped to the front of the

stage, held up his tattered Bible, and said, "The Word did not become printer's ink; it became grace and truth." I thought, "Aha! Jesus is the Word!" It was a life-changing experience. It was probably my life's most mystical moment as if a light came on and I realized I could no longer be a Fundamentalist. From that night, perfecting grace did not mean a combative, argumentative posture that berates anyone who disagrees. Rather it meant in the words of St. Paul, being "in Christ."

"Unlearning" began immediately. I was a pastor, preaching every Sunday. I was a seminary student at Duke Divinity School, listening to lectures, writing papers, and riding a hundred and twenty-six miles five days a week in a carpool with seminary classmates. In that context, I had to "unlearn" and re-think. That has been the premise of my journey for the past sixty-three years. Many times on many subjects with a diversity of people, I have had to recall my indelible image of hearing the saintly E. Stanley Jones in 1955.

Somewhere along my Christian journey, I discovered E. Stanley Jones' autobiographical testimony:

"I came to Christ bankrupt. My capacity to blunder drove me to his feet, and to my astonishment he took me, forgave me, and sent my happy soul singing. By grace was I saved, through faith, and that not of myself. It was a gift of God. I walked in the joy of that for months and then the clouds began to gather. There was something within me not redeemed, something else down in the cellar that seemed to be sullenly at war with this new life. I was at war with myself. I think I can see what happened. We live in two minds – the conscious and the subconscious."

The subconscious is the residing place of driving instincts – self, sex, and herd (peer pressure, desire to belong). These instincts have come down through a long racial history and they bend us toward evil. Into the conscious mind, there is introduced and at the time of conversion a new life, a new loyalty, a new love. But the subconscious mind does not obey this new life. Its driving instincts drive for fulfillment apart from the conscious mind. There ensues a clash between the new life in the conscious mind and the instincts of the subconscious. The house of soul becomes a house divided against itself. I wondered if that were the best that Christianity could do – to leave one in this divided condition.

I found to my glad surprise the teaching concerning the Holy Spirit, and I found that the area of the work of the Holy Spirit is largely, if not entirely, in the subconscious. I found that if I would surrender this conscious mind to the Holy Spirit – all I knew about it and all I did not know – He would cleanse at these depths that I could not control.

I surrendered and accepted the gift by faith. He did cleanse as a refining fire. In that cleansing there was a unifying. Conscious and subconscious were brought under a single control and redemption. That control was the Holy Spirit. I was no longer at war in myself. Life was on a permanently higher level. The soul had caught its stride. I went on my way singing a new song. That song has continued. It is fresher today than then." [212]

For Dr. Jones, that baptism of the Holy Spirit came instantaneously after years of struggle. For me, there was no "God moment" of that suddenness or magnitude. Instead I plodded on with the help of scholars like Albert Outler of Southern Methodist University, Harry Denman of the Methodist General Board of Evangelism, and one sermon by John Killinger. "Unlearning" is much more difficult and downright painful than learning. Perfecting grace is very, very different from a spirit of fundamentalism that can be the relational attitude of either a conservative or a liberal. Either posture can be snobbish, hortatory, and condescending. Perfecting grace leads us to be gracious, kind, humble, and serving.

That was over sixty years ago. The Holy Spirit became consciously my spiritual watchdog through which I examine

212 Internet.

my soul for sins of thought, word, and deed. Across the decades of time and the ups and downs of my vocational journey and personal life, I have come to embrace an understanding of Christian perfection as the deep yearning of my soul. My ongoing challenge has been and is to "have the mind which was in Christ Jesus" and to respond wholly to the will of God as we understand it with the result that sin loses both its grip and its appeal.

I find inspiration in Psalm 42 {NIV}:

"As the deer pants for streams of water, so my soul pants for you, my God. My soul thirsts for God, for the living God. When can I go and meet with God?... Deep calls to deep in the roar of your waterfalls; all your waves and breakers have swept over me... By day the Lord directs his love, at night his song is with me – a prayer to the God of my life" (selected verses).

I do sometimes ask with the psalmist, "Why are you cast down O my soul and why are you so disturbed within me?" Perhaps almost everyone has this "dark night of the soul"; even Mother Teresa wrote in her diary that she did. But in my older years, I am developing more and more the confidence of the author of Psalm 130 {NIV}: "I wait for the Lord, my whole being waits, and in his word I put my hope. I wait for the Lord more than watchmen wait for the morning...." (vss. 5-6)

My greatest guides are those to which we turn in the next chapter–spiritual disciplines that Wesley called "means of grace." As I have turned the corners in career and age or other changes in life, I prayed for the renewal of my journey of seeking God's perfecting grace. With each turn of "Pilgrim Road," Brian Wren speaks to me in his hymn:

"This is a day of new beginnings, time to remember and move on

Time to believe what love is bringing, Laying to rest the pain that's gone.

Christ is alive and goes before us to show and share what love can do

This is a day of new beginnings, our God is making all things new." [213]

Perfecting grace is identifying with Paul's confession to the Philippians:

> "Work out your salvation with fear and trembling... Not that I have already reached my goal, but I press on to make it my own because Christ has made me his own... But one thing I do: Forgetting what is behind and straining toward what is ahead."
>
> **Philippians 3:12-13 {NIV}**

An old gospel hymn, ***"Higher Ground,"*** had the line,

> *"I'm pressing on the upward way, new heights I'm gaining every day;*
>
> *Still praying as I'm onward bound, 'Lord plant my feet on higher ground.'*
>
> *My heart has no desire to stay where doubts arise and fears dismay;*
>
> *Tho' some may dwell where these abound, 'Lord plant my feet on higher ground.'"*

The Holy Spirit continues to whisper to our heart, to nudge our conscience, and to lead us to new insights. The never ending journey leads us to renewed and new relationships, readings, and means of grace.

Listening to Contemporary Wesleyan Voices on Perfecting Grace

Bishop Ken Carder reminds us that "grace is not content to give us a new status before God; it creates in us a new being...." [214] He continues, "We are surrounded by grace which prods,

---

213 Op. Cit., Young, *UMC Hymnal*, 383.

214 Op. Cit., Carder, 63.

prompts, purges, and perfects us in love." [215]

His wisdom continues with this statement: "As prevenient grace is that which God does before us, justifying grace is what God does for us, sanctifying grace is what God does in us. These do not affirm human potential as much as the power of God." [216]

Jason Vickers, a former faculty colleague, and now a professor at Asbury Theological Seminary's Memphis campus, reflects Wesley's definition of sanctification as "love of God and love of neighbor" when he wrote, "Wesley regarded entire sanctification or Christian perfection as having above all to do with the filling of the human heart with love for God and neighbor and the governing of all subsequent thoughts, words, and deeds, by that love." [217]

Reinhold Niebuhr enlightened us on the difficulty of being a moral individual in a society tainted by sin. Walter Muelder has written, "Twentieth century holiness envisages a whole person in a whole society." [218] In the late-twentieth century, Methodism not only recovered Wesley's insistence on "grace upon grace" or perfecting grace, but we also recovered his insistence that there "is no holiness but social holiness."

In Bishop Ken Carder's book *Living Our Beliefs,* he points out our tendency to interpret sin through our provincial cultures; thus, we are blinded from "seeing ourselves as others see us" (to quote Robert "Bobby" Burns). Sanctification must be seen from a higher plane than parish, region, nation, race, gender, income, and denomination. It must have a social justice component, a dimension of influencing the culture that was missing in so much of our Christian history, allowing us to claim sanctification while accommodating our treatment of

---

215 Ibid., 66.

216 Ibid, 63.

217 Vickers, Jason, *The Cambridge Companion to John Wesley,* Cambridge Press, 2010, 205.

218 Muelder, Walter, *"Ethics and the Interior Life,"* New Christian Advocate, June, 1957, 18-22.

Native Americans, Japanese Americans in World War II, African Americans in slavery and segregation, women in a myriad of subtle ways, and persons of alternative lifestyles. While the "people groups" were different in Jesus' day, we need to itemize the disenfranchised, ostracized, and criticized with whom Jesus engaged, relieved, and included.

There's one thing every Christian has in common – that Jesus has said, "Follow me." I long ago memorized the words of Albert Schweitzer:

> "He comes to us as one unknown just as on the shore of the lake. He approached those men who knew him not. His words are the same: 'Follow thou Me!' and He puts us to the tasks He has to carry out in our age. He commands. And to those who obey, be they wise or simple, He will reveal Himself in the fellowship of peace and activity, of struggle and suffering, till they come to know, as an inexpressible secret, Who He is." [219]

Kurt Kaiser and Ralph Carmichael published a gospel song in the sixties that speaks to and for me:

> *"I wish for you my friend this happiness that I've found;*
>
> *You can depend on God; it matters not where you're bound*
>
> *I'll shout it from the mountaintop. I want the world to know*
>
> *The Lord of love has come to me; I want to pass it on.*
>
> *Once you've experienced it, you want to sing*
>
> *It 's fresh like spring, you want to pass it on."*

To grow in grace, to be discipled into the "mind that was in Christ Jesus," to "go on to perfection" by ways that Wesley outlined what he called the "means of grace." To those we now turn.

---

219 Schweitzer, Albert, *Out My Life and Thought*, Johns Hopkins University Press, 1933, 59.

Questions for Discussion and Reflection

Within The United Methodist Church, have you ever heard
taught or preached the "doctrine of sanctification?" Have you
heard it in another church during your journey? To you is
this a new concept of grace?

Did you find this chapter helpful?

Do you feel yourself "drawn" to a personal journey of perfecting
grace, or does it "put you off?"

To either answer, "Why? What attracts you? What repels you?"

Are you threatened by the metaphor of God's walking you
through your "house" of relationships, opinions, and temptations to which you habitually yield? Do you fear that God will
ask you to unpack your prejudices, biases, and denigrating
expressions regarding some people groups?

If you desire to "grow in grace," you are now ready to move
to the next chapter on Wesley's "means of grace!" These are
disciplines that John Wesley used and recommended for us to
experience "grace upon grace."

"What are the 'means' ordained by God as the usual channels of his grace?" "Christ is the only means of grace, but the means by which the grace is conveyed are prayer, searching the Scriptures, and receiving the Lord's Supper."

John Wesley

"By 'means of grace' I understand outward signs, words, or actions ordained of God and appointed to be the ordinary channels whereby God might convey to us preventing, justifying, or sanctifying grace."

John Wesley

"The number of those who have abused the ordinances of God is far greater than the number of those who despised them."

John Wesley

"Religion that God our Father accepts as pure and faultless is this: to look after orphans and widows in their distress and to keep oneself from being polluted by the world. What good is it, my brothers and sisters, if someone claims to have faith but has no deeds? Can such faith save them? In the same way, faith by itself, if it is not accompanied by action, is dead."

James 1:27; 2:14, 17 (NIV)

"Your Word is a lamp to my feet and a light for my path."

–Psalm 119:105 (NIV)

"Now fear the Lord and serve him with all faithfulness. Throw away the gods your ancestors worshiped beyond the Euphrates River and in Egypt, and serve the Lord. But if serving the Lord seems undesirable to you, then choose for yourselves this day whom you will serve, whether the gods your ancestors served beyond the Euphrates, or the gods of the Amorites, in whose land you are living. But as for me and my household, we will serve the Lord."

Joshua 24:14-15 {NIV}

"Every year Jesus' parents went to Jerusalem for the Festival of the Passover. He went to Nazareth, where he had been brought up, and on the Sabbath day he went into the synagogue, as was his custom..."

Luke 2:41; 4:16 {NIV}

"They devoted themselves to the apostles' teaching and to fellowship, to the breaking of bread and to prayer."

Acts 2:42 {NIV}

"For I received from the Lord what I also passed on to you. The Lord Jesus on the night when he was betrayed took bread and when he had given thanks, he broke it and said .... In the same way, after supper, he took the cup also, ...For whenever you eat this bread and drink this cup, you proclaim the Lord's death until he comes."

I Corinthians 11:23-24a, 25a, 26 {NIV}

"When they had sung a hymn, they went out to the Mount of Olives. ...They went to a place called Gethsemane, and Jesus said to the disciples, 'Sit here while I pray."

Mark 14:26, 32 {NIV}

"Your Word is a lamp to my feet and a light for my path."

Psalm 119:105 {NIV}

Chapter Ten

Some "Means of Grace"
for Keeping in Touch with God

"...You have turned away from my decrees and have not kept them."

Malachi 3:7 {NIV}

The overall theme of this book is God's grace. We have documented the triune ways in which God manifests grace to us, but what are the channels through which grace is conveyed? Certainly people are different and many report visions of a rather sensational nature, but most of us are "soldiers in the kingdom," following the gleam like the shepherds and wise men did. Personally, I am not very mystical. I love the words of George Croly, vicar of a small Anglican parish:

"I ask no dream, no prophet ecstasies,

No sudden rending of this veil of clay,

No angel visitant, no opening skies.

But take the dimness of my soul away."

Like many of us, Wesley grew up in the church and even as a child began to learn scripture verses, say evening prayers and hear his parents pray table grace. He was baptized as an infant in St. Andrews Anglican Church in Epworth, Lincolnshire, England where his father was a parish priest. Like many clergy, he felt God's call to ordained ministry while he was in college.

For thirteen years (1725-38), he read deeply in the writings of saints who urged every Christian to be very disciplined, to practice acts of Christian mercy, and certainly to "attend the ordinances of God." By the term "ordinance" they meant the worship services of the local church. During this chapter of his life, he practiced what he always called "holiness of heart and life." In this time of his spiritual journey he lacked the assurance of his personal salvation and the "peace which passes understanding." He came to that experience through the mentoring of the Moravians, first aboard ship headed to Georgia, later in Georgia, and still later, in the spring of 1738, back in England.

With all his indebtedness to the Moravians, he felt increasingly ill at ease with their understanding of grace as quietism with no means of grace. Their "golden text" of the entire Bible was, "Be still and know that I am God." According to Rupert Davies, a superb British Methodist historian, "They interpreted Psalm 46:10 to mean that 'stillness' is abstention from Holy Communion, corporate worship Bible reading, corporate prayer or even good works until the Christian were perfectly sanctified." [220]

They insisted that they should "lie still at Jesus' feet" until they had an emotionally cleansing experience of faith. They insisted that until a person had "full assurance of faith," they should not take Communion nor practice any works of mercy. They did not believe in any "degrees of faith," but Wesley thought otherwise and taught "growth in grace."

Wesley disagreed with those who negate the years of our spiritual journey when we followed Christ "from a distance." He called this "weak faith" but did not negate it. Wesley said point-blank to the Moravians, "There are degrees of faith. A man may have some degree of it before all things in him become new – before he has the full assurance of faith, the abiding witness of the Spirit, or the clear perception that Christ dwelleth in him." [221] He referred to Paul's letter to the Corinthi-

---

220 Op. Cit., Davies, 66.

221 Op. Cit. Outler, *John Wesley,* Oxford Press, 1964, 356.

ans, "I fed you with milk, not solid food, for you were not ready for solid food." (1 Co. 3:2 {NIV}) Eighteen months after the Moravians had "midwifed" Wesley's experience of "knowing his sins forgiven" at Aldersgate, he could no longer abide their doctrine of "stillness."

Wesley insisted that Christianity cannot be a "solitary religion." He was still and forever would be an Anglican, "opposed with all his might any disparagement of the 'means of grace.'" [222] He broke with the Moravians because he insisted that "weak faith" can be strengthened by the means of grace, which the church alone supplies. He said, "I believe it is right for him who knows not faith to go to church, commune, pray, read the Scripture, do all the temporal good he can and endeavour after doing spiritual good." [223]

He would not, indeed he could not, negate his years of leading the Holy Club at Oxford, where they ministered to prisoners, organized daycare for children, fed the poor, and insisted, "There is no holiness without social holiness." He insisted that ethics is the fruit of faith and he abhorred any doctrine that "allows a believer to have a passive attitude toward either the means of grace or the demand of the Gospel for actual righteousness." [224]

By July 20, 1740, the final break came when the Methodists left the Moravians forever. Wesley said conclusively:

"There are means of grace, i.e. outward ordinances, whereby the inward grace of God is ordinarily conveyed to man before the faith that brings salvation. One of these means is the Lord's Supper. He who has not faith should wait for it through the use of this and other means by which God hath ordained." [225]

---

222 Op. Cit., Davies, 66.

223 Op. Cit., Outler, *John Wesley,* 357-358.

224 Ibid., 347.

225 Wesley, Sermon, "The Means of Grace," JWW, Vol. 1, 376-377.

By the discipline of these means, we are encouraged to pursue the "high calling which is ours in Christ." Unlike Martin Luther and Moravian Bishop Spandenberg, John Wesley loved the book of James! Wesley's converts were no "rope of sand," but a connected, disciplined "order" of bands, class meetings, and societies. In each of them, Methodists were urged to develop the disciplines called "means of grace." Therefore, these are not the foundation but they are the capstone of Methodist fundamentals.

William Abraham helps us clarify that while Wesley's first concern was the salvation of souls, he insisted that God had supplied various means for the reception of grace, and most of those means are standard practices of your local church! [226] The reality is that for those of us who grew up in Christian homes, went to Sunday School and church, and made early commitments to Christ, the "means of grace" nurtured us in the faith until we, like Wesley, had our own "Aldersgate" experience. Without the church, we would be spiritual orphans.

Wesley's enunciating "means of grace" were his bulwark against two concerns:

- As the Methodist revival in England began seeing people's lives radically changed, Wesley had to urge the preachers to guard against what in that day was called "enthusiasm." Today we would call it emotionalism.

- We cannot retain "a spiritual high." We get in a "funk." Thomas a Kempis once wrote, "I have never found anyone so religious and devout that he had not sometimes a withdrawing of grace or felt not some decrease of zeal." [227]

Wesley was convinced that "inward and spiritual grace" needed intermittent and repetitive "outward and visible signs." We suffer from pain, grief, job loss, relationship betrayal, church disenchantment, and spiritual sloth. The means of grace – the Bible, prayer, church attendance, Holy Communion,

---

226 Op. Cit., Abraham, *Wesley for Armchair Theologians*, 111.

227 á Kempis, Thomas, *The Imitation of Christ*, Revell, 1953, 47.

holy conversation with trusted friends – can keep us from falling prey to the "dark night of the soul."

Wesley was forced to admit one "Achilles Heel" of the means of grace. They could become "ends" rather than only means. As Wesley closed his sermon entitled "The Means of Grace," he warned:

> "Before you use any means let it be deeply impressed on your soul: There is no power in this. It is in itself a poor, dead, empty thing; separate from God, it is a dry leaf, a shadow. Settle this in your heart; that there is no power to save but in the Spirit of God; consequently even what God ordains conveys no grace to the soul if you trust not in him alone." [228]

He reminds us, "Seek God alone. Every outward thing must be infused by the power of the Holy Spirit and the merits of Jesus. Nothing short of God can satisfy your soul." He preached, "External worship is lost labour without a heart devoted to God." [229]

Again, mutual heritage of "strangely warm heart" and means of grace make us a church of the "middle way."

In Albert Outler's 1974 Fondren lectures at Southern Methodist University, he morphed his lifetime of scholarly Wesleyan study into a rather folksy presentation. In his last lecture, he summarized Wesley's doctrine of holiness with his logic: "We have faith in order to love, we love in order to be good, we are good in order to be happy – all of which is what God made us for in this world and the next. This is 'holy living' as John Wesley saw it."

Discipline is really liberating. We too often think of John Wesley as being overly serious and seldom happy. To the contrary, according to his admirers and critics alike, Wesley had a strange, insistent reality of cheerfulness, joy, and high

---

228 Wesley, John, Sermon: "The Means of Grace," Vol. 1, , JWW, 396.

229 Ibid. Sermon: "The Means of Grace," 397.

spirits. He was, in Outler's words, "a happy man." Outler identified fifty-four quotes in which Wesley paired "happy" with "holy." He died happy, singing, praying, and with the words on his lips, "Best of all, God is with us." We would do well to follow his model of spiritual discipline as a means of conquering many of our human infirmities, channeling our energies into outward works of righteousness, and ending our struggle with unforgiven sins and unresolved guilt.

In Wesley's language about perfecting grace, he always used the verb, "'going' on to perfection" which implies a journey. The means of grace are the spiritual disciplines which support us through our seasons of life and our personal circumstances lest we either grow weary in well doing or yield to temptations. An old gospel song affirmed this: "Ask the Savior to help you, comfort, strengthen, and keep you, He is willing to aid you; He will carry you through." In the old fashioned "testimony meetings," the recent convert, whose conversion brought with it a radically new lifestyle, would often close his or her testimony before the older Christians, "Pray for me that I will hold out faithful."

If we are to grow in "taming our bears," "caging our lions," and knowing our purpose, we must have some spiritual discipline. By practicing the means of grace, we can attain the faithful courage to say "no" to sins of the flesh and sins of the spirit that entice us. We can practice the presence of God and see love overcome fear. We can attain a lifestyle that combines responsibility with freedom and freedom with responsibility. Just as Paul said, "I can do all things through Christ who strengthens me." (Phil. 4:13 {NIV})

John Wesley's was a "practical divinity." Bishop Bevel Jones used to love the doggerel: "The main thing is to keep the main thing the main thing." An old gospel hymn had us sing, "Keep your eyes upon Jesus." Paul urged us to "let the mind be in you which was in Christ Jesus." The world into which John Wesley sought to bring some ordering of private lives, some decency in human behavior, some peace to domestic violence, and some growth in personal grace was not a pretty world. It was the world that Charles Dickens described in his books like *Oliver Twist*. Methodism was a movement among the masses—men who drank too much at the pub, women who were shrews, abused children who became abusers when they had children.

Therefore, I encourage you, dear reader, whatever your age, life stage, or psychological disposition to practice Wesley's means of grace. Do not fall prey to the cultural mythology that "being spiritual" will make you morbid or a wimp. Christian discipleship empowers us with faithful courage. Let us turn now to John Wesley's regimen of spiritual disciplines that he called "means of grace." He lists three as the "chief means": Prayer, Searching the Scriptures, and the Lord's Supper. Others he adds in several settings as distinctive ways and means to "keep our heart in tune with the Infinite."

Wesley's Means of Grace

#1: Prayer, whether in secret or the great congregation

Jesus' disciples noticed how much prayer meant in Jesus' life. One day, they asked him, "Lord, teach us to pray." Our prayer life is often either a sleepy routine at night, a sentence prayer at the stop light, or a "foxhole prayer" when we are "under fire." Like the "Twelve," we need to ask in our own journey, "Teach me to pray." I love the concept of prayer in James Montgomery's words in 1818:

"Prayer is the soul's sincere desire, unuttered or expressed,

The motion of a hidden fire that trembles in the breast.

Prayer is the burden of a sigh, the falling of a tear,

The upward glancing of an eye, when none but God is near."

Let us practice beginning our prayers with meditation on a recent scene of beauty in creation, or the music of a great choir, or some other reminder of God's majesty. I begin often with Psalm 103:1 {NIV}: "Praise the Lord, my soul; all my inmost being, praise his holy name." This moves us out of our own little world and mentally into the presence of the Creator. Then, unless we are in a crisis moment, let us be careful to "count our blessings" before we move to our burdens. Giving thanks for what gives us an "attitude of gratitude." It at least balances our complaining about what is not the way we wish it were!

Naturally, we are going to ask for God to help us in our life situation, but prayers of petition must not monopolize our prayers, making the Lord God Almighty our personal errand boy. Intercessory prayer is powerful; it gives God a chance to call us to be the "loving heart" or the "act of kindness" that is needed by the person or situation for which we are praying. Our motive is concern, not ordering the Almighty to do his homework! We must caution against being too casual with our promise, "I'll pray for you." They may need a hug, a phone call, a card, or a sandwich for their next meal. We can so easily make a casual promise to pray for someone and simply forget! If we have committed ourselves to the sacred covenant of inter-cessory prayer, we must remember!

Lastly, we need to do our own spiritual housecleaning, asking God to empower us to do what we cannot do alone – to forgive, to have faithful courage, to overcome fear, to "kick" habits, and to trust God as one who loves us.

Because I am a person afflicted with insomnia, I close my nighttime prayer by asking for release from the burdens and stress of the day followed by a slow, meditative recitation of the 23rd Psalm. It is my guide into God's will, followed by God's promises.

At the lowest moment of my life, after a sleepless night in Kansas City in the winter of 1980, I had a "God moment" when I reached that long familiar line: "He maketh me to lie down in green pastures." I had always concentrated on the green pastures and skipped the predicate! That night/morning I real-ized that sometimes because God loves us, God has to discipline us. I had to be made to lie down before I could get Don out of the driver's seat, and look up to God as the "rod and staff" who would lead me through the valley, deliver me from fear of evil, fill my cup, and anoint my head with the "balm of Gilead" that "makes the wounded whole and cures the sin-sick soul."

Another dimension of prayer that has become increasingly meaningful for me is the rich mine of prayers and hymns from the Church across the ages. I have sprinkled hymn quotes throughout this book. I mention here two prayers from medieval church liturgy. One is the "Prayer of Humble Access:"

"We do not presume to come to this, Thy Table, trusting in our own righteousness but in Thy manifold and great mercies. We are not worthy so much as to gather up the crumbs under Thy table, but Thou are the same Lord whose nature is always to have mercy."

The other is the "Collect for Purity:"

"Almighty God, unto whom all hearts are open, all desires known, and from whom no secrets are hid; cleanse the thoughts of our hearts by the inspiration of Thy Holy Spirit, that we may perfectly love Thee and worthily magnify Thy Holy Name."

These prayers I have long ago committed to memory and in many life situations find them more helpful than to "ad lib" in talking with my Father who art in heaven.

#2: Searching the Scriptures

Paul wrote to young Timothy, "All Scripture is God-breathed and is useful for teaching, rebuking, correcting and training in righteousness" (II Timothy 3:16 {NIV}).[230] The sense of the term "means of grace" is certainly implied in this text. The saddest plight of spiritual poverty for most Christians is biblical illiteracy. The reason we so easily fall prey to false

---

230 Op. Cit., Wesley, *Explanatory Notes Upon the New Testament*, 794.

doctrines is that people manipulate the Scriptures and play biblical hopscotch, and we have not mastered the Bible enough to counter those who confuse us.

Memorizing favorite scripture verses is a great practice, but isolated verses are like a string of pearls! Before we can properly hear God's word, we need to learn what is called the "meta–narrative" or the "macro" view of the whole of scripture. Even the best of sermons are seldom good teachers of the Bible. Sunday School lessons play what I call "biblical hop-scotch," jumping from one isolated group of verses to another. The sad result is that our lack of biblical mastery is rather embarrassing.

Methodist "Article of Religion #V" reads, "The Holy Scriptures containeth all things necessary for salvation." Then the Article lists all the books of the present biblical canon. "The Bible is the Word of God, inspired in its writing and intended for "reproof, correction, and training in righteousness."(II Timothy 3:16 {NIV}) Its overarching message is redemptive.

We must search the Scriptures for language, cultural context, theological context, and style of literature, but we must never lose sight of Scripture as "the Word of God for the people of God." With all the good benefits of biblical criticism since the mid-19th century, scholars have often dissected the Bible and never put it together again! That is like a surgeon who would remove our organs for examining, then not put us together again! Wesley deliberately used the term "Searching the scriptures." This does not mean a casual reading or giblets of inspiration, but a systematic study. Searching the Scripture is different from academic Bible study or sermon preparation.

We must pore over the Word and pray over the Word until the Spirit speaks to us through the words! Charles Wesley is our best teacher here:

"Whether the Word be preached or read, no saving benefit I gain

From empty sounds or letters dead, unprofitable all and vain

Unless by faith thy word I hear and see its heavenly character.

If God enlighten through his Word, I shall my kind Enlightener bless;

But void and naked of my Lord, what are all verbal promises?

Nothing to me, till faith divine, inspire, inspeak, and make them mine."

"Search the Scripture" –tools, techniques, and procedures

Select a place to which you will go to study. Keep your "library" there. It is your "Upper Room" though it may be a closet or a stump by the spring in the woods. Begin your study wherever you believe to be the most spiritually helpful at this point in your journey.

Adopt a personal discipline of how many chapters you will read per day and stick with it.

Use one biblical translation as your "home base," but have at least two others to consult if you "get stuck." The New Revised Standard Version and the New International Version are printed parallel in "The New Interpreter's Bible." Both reflect good work from the Hebrew and Greek texts. Use paraphrases sparingly as your basic biblical text – "The Living Bible," "The Good News Bible," "The Message" etc.

Read your daily passage slowly, sometimes word by word. Stop and meditate on its meaning. Read it aloud if possible. Flora Wuellner compares this to soaking in a tub of warm water, and letting our body absorb the calming, cleansing effects of the water. Pray the words of Charles Wesley: "Unlock the truth, thyself the key, unseal the sacred book."

Buy a one volume commentary or "companion" to the Bible. One is my own: *Reading the Bible Again and Seeing It for the First Time* that is available from Amazon.

Commit some verses, or chapters, to memory if you can. One day you might be blind or disabled by a stroke or wired up following a car accident and you cannot hold a Bible! You also have nights you cannot sleep, or times you must sit and wait. The psalmist said, "On thy law I meditate day and night."

Amend these suggestions in any way that suits you best!!

3. The Lord's Supper

Of all the strengths of frontier Methodism, the greatest loss was the spiritual grace associated with the sacrament of the Lord's Supper. Only the African-American children of Wesley kept the sanctity and theology of Wesley regarding Holy Communion. Most rural churches moved the Lord's Supper to quarterly usage and casual spirituality. Indeed, for generations, there was lower attendance when communion was served than when "the preacher was preaching." That is not Wesleyan. Wesley insisted:

- That "The Lord's Supper was ordained by God to be a means of conveying to [men] either preventing or sancti-fying grace, according to their several necessities."

- That the persons for whom it was ordained are those who know and feel they want the grace of God either to affirm or re-affirm forgiveness for their sins, or to empower them through the Holy Spirit to resist their temptations to sin.

- That there is no previous preparation necessary but a desire to receive whatsoever he pleases to give.

- That no fitness or membership is required at the time of communing but a sense of our state or need. That is, the rail shall be open to any and all which feel led to commune.

We will never know the full meaning of the Lord's Supper on this side of heaven, but in recent years, considerable consensus has developed around two terms–a "holy mystery" of the Holy Spirit's ministering to us, and the "real presence" of Christ. The Eucharist is indeed a means of grace we neglect to our spiritual peril. Wesley cited I Corinthians 10:16, then commented, "Is not the eating of that bread, and the drinking of that cup, the outward, visible means whereby God conveys into our souls all that spiritual grace, that righteousness, and peace and joy of the Holy Ghost which were purchased by the body once broken and the blood once shed for us? Let all, therefore, who truly desire the grace of God, eat of that bread and drink of that cup." [231]

In his sermon, "The Means of Grace," Wesley listed only Prayer, Searching the Scriptures, and The Lord's Supper as what he called the "chief means" of grace. However, in other times, sermons, tracts, etc. he felt led to enumerate other occasions that God uses to inspire us with "grace upon grace."

4. Holy Conversation

The entire cultural history of the West has made us loners. Almost every facet of our lives discourage trust and soul-sharing. Even in marriage, so many couples realize when the children are grown that the two adults who once married each other no longer know each other! We not only need a friend in Jesus, we need Jesus' friends. A profound insight of William Young in *The Shack* is Mack's asking Papa, Jesus, and Sarayu (who are his depiction of the Trinity), "Who's in charge? Don't you have a chain of command?" Jesus answers, "Chain of command? That sounds ghastly."

> Sarayu (the Holy Spirit) comments, "We are in a circle of relationship, not a chain of command. Humans are so lost and damaged that to you it is almost incomprehensible that people could work together or live together without someone being in charge. This is why experiencing true relationship [with God] is so difficult." [232]

At another point, Papa tells Mack, "It is all about love and relationship. All love and relationship is possible for you only because it already exists within Me, within God myself. Love is not the limitation; love is like the bird's flying. I am love." (As if on cue, the little bird on the windowsill flew up, up, and away!) [233]

---

231 Ibid. 615.

232 Op. Cit., Young 122.

233 Ibid., 101.

During his Georgia missionary pastorate, Wesley's diary is sprinkled with almost daily references to time spent in "necessary talk" or "holy conversation." He eventually included this in some of his lists of "means of grace." In recent times this term has been morphed into "holy conferencing." "Holy Conferencing" or Holy conversation has two dimensions. One is reflected in the old adage, "great minds talk about ideas, average minds talk about events, and small minds talk about people." Our lives are so enriched when we hear speeches and sermons or develop relationships that push our minds to new horizons and our soul to greater depths. In today's cybernetic world, we risk overloading our minds in trivia and junk. Much of today's headlines is tomorrow's trash. Holy conversation you can recall years later as profound insight from a colleague.

In his sermon, "The Means of Grace," Wesley encourages those of us who are more mature to reach out to the "babes in Christ" and the seekers. "Thus we may lead him step by step through all the means which God has ordained; not according to our own will, but just as providence and the Spirit of God go before and open the way."

My mother often told me, "You are known by the company you keep." Though she meant my reputation – and the likelihood of being influenced by bad habits such as smoking, drinking, and using profanity – at a much deeper level, her advice is still more correct. If we hang out with people who are reading, thinking, praying, doing justice, loving mercy, and walking humbly with God, we will likely adopt that lifestyle and discipline as our own.

There is a deeper dimension in "holy conversation." This is the need to have a trusted confidant. Carlyle Marney, founder of a clergy retreat center called "Interpreters' House," wrote a significant book called *Priests to Each Other.*

I transposed that years ago into "priest at your elbow" and preached a sermon by that title. More people asked for copies than almost any sermon I ever preached. The response taught me how lonely people are and convinced me that every Christian needs "a priest." This might well not be a clergyperson and certainly does not mean our need for a confessional booth in a church! This means someone with whom one can exchange the journey of souls, the peaks and valleys, the doubts and fears, the joys, and God-moments. Some movements urge the term and formality of "spiritual director." We need not get so technical–just someone we trust and can really be honest with!

Dr. Marney insisted that this should not be your spouse. That raises a word of caution. Your "priest" must be a person with whom we do not cross sexually tempting boundaries. Marney urged pastors not to choose another pastor of the same denomination. We always run the risk of betrayal, and denominational colleagues are more apt to yield to that temptation!

The point is that "the heart is a lonely hunter" and we need to find someone who is not as an intermediary with God but a confidant. If holy conversation is the essence of these relationships, it is not our becoming more like the other, but both becoming more like Jesus.

Leonard Sweet has written an important book called simply, *11*. He takes eleven biblical characters, gives them psychological/theologically descriptive titles, and advises that each of us needs the counterpart of a Nathan, the prophet, who will tell us what we need to know about our sins, a Jonathan who will be a true friend, a Barnabas who will be the "encourager," a "little one" like Rhoda, some "VIP's" like Lydia and Lazarus, and a sacred place like "Jerusalem." From these relationships come many holy conversations.

Sweet always sprinkles his books with pregnant quotes, one of which in this book is from psychologist and author Larry Crabb: "The Church is a community of people on a journey to God." [234]

I often hear from clergy the sad words, "I have many acquaintances and no real friends." Sweet cites Mark's word about Jesus: "He appointed twelve, that they might be with him." (Mark 3:14 {NIV}) If Jesus needed twelve, why do we Christians think we can go it alone? Sweet describes God's "dream

---

234 Sweet, Leonard, *11*, David C. Cook, 2008, 17.

team" as the "Triple F's" – Faithful Friends Forever.[235]

I think Wesley was onto something that might be even more necessary in the twenty-first century than it was in the eighteenth–the class meeting. Until the 1850s, those small groups were the essential socio-spiritual vehicle for Methodists. The Sunday School system unintentionally replaced it. Today, Sunday School is in a slow death spiral. We need to re-invent some version of the class meeting. We need holy conversation!

5.Fasting

Wesley fasted. Every Wednesday and Friday, he ate nothing until the afternoon traditional English "tea time." He saw food as fuel to provide him energy for his work, not as an indulgence to be enjoyed for its own sake. He never encouraged fasting to the point of harming one's health, but did see it as a spiritual discipline; indeed, as a means of grace.

For the most part, Methodism has neither taught nor practiced fasting as a means of grace. With the increasingly serious problem of obesity in Europe and North America, we need to look anew at the stewardship of the body. Fasting undoubtedly is needed to cleanse the body of toxins. Our diet has far too many food additives, sugar substitutes, and trans fats. Fast foods and low activity levels are creating a generation of children who will have major health issues. If we do not see fasting per se as a means of grace, we certainly need to see temperance at the table as a means of health –physical, emotional, and spiritual.

6. Participation in a Church

In Wesley's lifetime, he never acknowledged Methodism as a church; to him it was a movement of renewal within the Church of England. He never allowed Methodist societies to meet at "church hours." He insisted that a "means of grace" was the Sunday worship service of the parish church. By the twentieth century, Sunday morning worship had become the major paradigm for "building up the saints" in all denominations. The

---

235 Ibid., 23.

church has no effective substitute for faith development.

"The Confession of Faith" of the former EUB church affirms that the "church is the community of all true believers under the Lordship of Christ...the redemptive fellowship in which the Word of God is preached by men divinely called, and the sacraments are duly administered.... Under the discipline of the Holy Spirit, the Church exists for the maintenance of worship, the edification of believers, and the redemption of the world."

Given this definition, the church belongs in this list as a "means of grace." Indeed God has used the Church, with all its human weaknesses, to be the vehicle of all the other means of grace, including Holy Scriptures.

Worship within the church lifts us beyond the church to God. Gothic architecture was designed to lift people beyond the misery, poverty, deaths, and other hardships of life in their parish. They sacrificed for centuries to build cathedrals to lift their thoughts, but now we must use other means. Music is a marvelous vehicle – both instrumental and vocal. So is preaching. Few exchanges in one's life surpass an honest preacher sharing with a congregation what he or she has experienced with God.

The sad mistake of the twentieth century was to develop a "church-ianity" that was not synonymous with "Christ-ianity." We developed "churchmanship" (male and female) rather than discipleship. We are overly affected by who the preacher/pastor is. We assimilate new members by placing them on finance committees and program teams when they were babes in Christ looking for soul nourishment. Finally, Sunday worship is not a setting for finding spiritual colleagues or friends.

Wesley's Final Word on 'Means'

"Remember also to use all means as means; as ordained, not for their own sake, but in order to the renewal of your soul...." We do humbly believe that John Wesley is a mentor of merit who can lead us to a life well-lived if we learn from what he called living by the "means of grace."

Questions for Discussion and Reflection

Do you agree that our enthusiasm about our faith and confidence in our beliefs will "leak out" if we do not practice some spiritual discipline?

St. Augustine reportedly once said, "Love God and do what you please." Some have equated this to the adage, "Let your conscience be your guide." In other words, "Different strokes for different folks." All of these sayings get us "off the hook" from spiritual disciplines. Wesley liked specificity in what he called "practical divinity." He also called it "holiness of heart and life" or simply "holy living."

What is your experience of and evaluation of Wesley's itemized "means of grace?"

Prayer – not what we say about it, but our real, honest to God practice

Searching the Scriptures – Seriously, how much "homework" have you done in learning what the Bible really says? If you took an "S.A.T." on the Bible, what would your score be?

Do you deeply regret it when you miss church on "Communion Sunday?" If you wrote the policy, how often would your church have communion? Has the spiritual value of communion increased or decreased in the last ten years?

Holy conversation – Do you see value in having what I call "a priest at your elbow" or what some call a "spiritual director?" Do you have a friend whom you totally trust? If not, do you wish you did?

Have you ever practiced fasting as a spiritual discipline? If so, evaluate it.

How many Sundays a year do you attend worship at a local church? How does this compare or contrast with ten years ago? Has your church attendance been substantially affected by who the preacher has been or is now?

What kind of books do you read?

Would you add other means of grace to Wesley's list? Which will you delete?

Which "means of grace" are the most meaningful for you in your own journey?

Which "means of grace" have you been most negligent of?

As you read this chapter, what decisions have you made about your own "means of grace?"

Chapter Eleven

Mr. Wesley's "Catholic Spirit"

John Wesley lived 1703-1791, a century unprecedented in sophistication. He was a contemporary of every major "history game changer" of the eighteenth century. It was the century called "Enlightenment" by those who considered monarchies and state churches as "dark." Charles Dickens defined the era as "the best of times, the worst of times."

Wesley had done his homework in the stacks of Oxford's thirty-seven college libraries. He was incredibly well read in an amazingly broad range of subjects. He read accounts of missionaries, sea captains, and travelers reflecting religion and culture on six continents. He read of their encounters with Muslims, Hindu, and Buddhists. In the libraries, he committed to memory some of the wisdom sayings of Confucius and the "Enlightened Paths" of the Buddha.

Obviously, he and the Deists did not think alike, but he read deeply in the works of Adam Smith, David Hume, John Locke – all of Scotland or England; and Montesquieu and Voltaire of France. He was an avid reader in the thirty-seven college librarites of Oxford University at the center of the British Empire in the Age of Enlightenment.

As a missionary in the American colony of Georgia, he was de facto pastor to Portuguese Jews, Italian Catholics, French Hugenots, German Palatinates, and Seminole Native Americans. He also was in weekly conversation with German Moravians and pastor to a quite diverse Anglican congregation. He was very much a man in touch with his time. This greatly affected what would become known as his "catholic spirit."

Since his times were one of the most seismic shifts in history for a lot of disciplines, his sermon, "Catholic Spirit," reflects our need to be broad minded in ways other than denominational differences. Join me in a short jaunt down "Changing Times Lane" during the age of the so called "Enlightenment."

In economic theory, guilds and government licensed monopolies which controlled the pricing and marketing of all goods and services. This was a major bone of contention with the American colonists until flashpoints like the Boston Tea Party evolved into armed rebellion. In 1776, Adam Smith, a professor of moral philosophy in Glasgow, Scotland, wrote what became, and should still be, the textbook for macro-economics – *An Inquiry Into the Nature and Cause of the Wealth of Nations*. John Wesley was a contemporary of Adam Smith.

In philosophy, the Anglican Church and its predecessor, the Roman Catholic Church, were losing control of what books could be published and what could be taught in the emerging universities. John Wesley read deeply in Scotland's David Hume who insisted that morality was not related to revealed religious truth, such as the Ten Commandments. In England, men like John Locke and Francis Bacon were fathers of "the age of reason." They rejected the miracle element in religion. Wesley saw the merits of reason, but not to the expense of revelation. Cambridge and Oxford were awash in the new findings of Isaac Newton who observed the power of gravity, invented the mathematics of calculus, and defined "Newtonian physics." Just across the channel the "fathers of the Enlightenment" were men like Rousseau with his philosophy of socialism, and Montesquieu who conceived a new paradigm of political science–the checks and balances in governmental power between three branches: executive, legislative, and judicial. James Madison patterned the United States Constitution after Montesquieu's political philosophy.

With the rise of the Puritan movement, British politics

and religion were blended. James I, a Presbyterian Scot whose mother was Catholic, was crowned king in 1603, became head of the Anglican Church, and stated that he would "harry the Puritans out of the land." His only olive branch to the Puritans was the King James Version of the Bible, but he was careful that only four of the fifty-three scholars were Puritans, and they were forced to sit on a long, wooden, backless bench while the Anglicans and Presbyterians sat in velvet covered chairs! The Puritans were dressed in plain clothes, the Presbyterians in plain robes, and the Anglicans in opulent vestments.

While King James told the Archbishop of Canterbury that he wanted "learned and grave men on both sides," the condescension and lack of civility was obvious. The men who gave us the King James Version were in sharp contrast to what John Wesley called for in his sermon, "The Catholic Spirit." One thing all the translators had in common – all were Calvinists. This bias shows up a lot in the old KJV!

In politics, "The Commonwealth" ruled Britain from 1642-1661 and was anything but an era where the people were taught religious pluralism. The Puritans finally formed an army that defeated the king's army and executed James' son, Charles I, in 1642. The victors executed King Charles I and established a theocracy in Britain under Puritan ("iron man") Oliver Cromwell. (1642-1658) He abolished all holy days including Christmas, removed all Christian symbols from the cathedrals, arrested maypole dancers in May, and encouraged the Baptists to re-baptize by immersion their children who had been baptized as infants. There was no mercy in England in the days of the Commonwealth.

The Restoration of the monarchy occurred four years after Cromwell's death. Puritans ("Dissenters") were driven from their pulpits, including Susanna Wesley's father and John Wesley's grandfather. The Anglican Church was restored in 1662 and Charles II was crowned as king. He was forced to abdicate after a reign of only six years and the "Glorious Revolution" in 1688 brought a new form of government to Great Britain – "parliamentary democracy." It was the end of absolute monarchy; the crown would be subject to the parliament. The corona-tion of William, a Dutchman, to the British throne was contro-versial even in the Wesley family and precipitated his parents being separated for over a year! The first child conceived after Samuel Wesley's return to Epworth from London was named "John" who would live almost the entirety of the momentous eighteenth century.

In religion, over 20,000 Puritans had left England between 1620 and 1642. They refused to use the King James Bible because it was too bawdy. They used the "Geneva Bible," often called the "breeches Bible" because the Puritan translators refused to portray Adam and Eve with fig leaves and portrayed them as wearing breeches! The Massachusetts Bay Colony, established in America, was a rigidly Calvinist theocracy, certainly not a faith community practicing "the catholic spirit" nor religious freedom.

Diarmaid MacCulloch, in his monumental, *Christianity – The First Three Thousand Years,* states and then documents that "by 1700 all the elements of the Enlightenment were in place." [236]

MacCulloch, son of an Anglican rector and Oxford profes-sor of history, paid quite a tribute to John Wesley :

"John Wesley, an intellectual omnivore himself, was deter-mined...to introduce his flocks to the excitement of knowl-edge and the achievements of natural philosophy. To do so, he published voluminously. One of the attractions of Meth-odism was its encouragement of self-education and self-im-provement among its flocks. Among his bestsellers was his handbook of practical medicine, *Primitive Physick.* He deplored the way in which the history of medicine depended upon Hypotheses, and reversed the process with Baconian empirical brio ("zest") in favour of remedies that could be

---

236 MacCulloch, Diarmaid, *Christianity – The First Three Thousand Years,* Viking, 2010, 794.

proved to work, although he coupled them with that 'Old, Unfashionable Medicine – Prayer.'" [237]

MacCulloch's tribute to Wesley from so famous a historian is significant, and it makes Wesley's Catholic Spirit more significant.

I have included this digest of seventeenth and eighteenth British history to refresh the memory of anyone who has forgotten one's knowledge of that era's conflicts, stress, and strife.

Preface to Wesley's Sermon: "The Catholic Spirit"

In another sermon, Wesley preached, "True religion is right tempers towards God and man. It is, in two words, gratitude and benevolence: gratitude to our Creator and supreme Benefactor, and benevolence to our fellow creatures. He pled to transfer our arguments about faith to our common ground of agreement. The sermon "Catholic Spirit" is, according to Albert Outler's analysis, "yet another statement of the essentials in an effort to reach a consensus." Dr. Outler continued, "Here, then, is a charter for a distinctive sort of doctrinal pluralism – one that stands at an equal distance from dogmatism on the one extreme and indifferentism on the other." [238]

Charles Wesley wrote a hymn that was published as an appendage to the sermon, "Catholic Spirit," when the two were published in 1770:

"Weary of all this worldly stife, these notions, forms, and modes and names,

To Thee, the Way, the Truth, the Life whose love my simple heart inflames;

Divinely taught, at last I fly, with thee and thine to live and die." [239]

---

237 Ibid., 795.

238 Op. Cit.,, Outler, JWW Vol. 2, 79-80.

239 Ibid., 80.

The sermon "Catholic Spirit" begins with a sad but accurate commentary on religious zealots who in Wesley's words interpreted love to "relation, acquaintance, friend," but "hate thine enemy."

Then he quoted Jesus: "You have heard that it was said, 'Love your neighbor and hate your enemy,' But I tell you: Love your enemies and pray for those who persecute you that you may appear to all mankind as children of your Father. He causes his sun to rise on the evil and the good, and sends rain on the righteous and the unrighteous." (Matthew 5:43-45 {NIV})

Wesley then quoted the Apostle John: "For this is the message that you heard from the beginning: We should love one another." (I John 3:11 {NIV}) This is Wesley's commentary on Jesus' summary of the law: "Love God...love neighbor..."

Wesley is often quoted as having said, "Methodists think and let think." That is taking part of a sentence out of context! He first enunciated what he considered to be his "essentials." He preached, "Every wise man therefore will allow the same liberty of thinking which he desires they should allow him; and will no more insist on their embracing his opinions than he would have them to insist on embracing theirs. He bears with those who differ from him." [240] He points to the bottom line of his premise: "Only one question is important and that is, 'Is thine heart right with me as mine is with Thee?" Then he enumerated what he called "opinions":

Mode of worship is an opinion often not shared with persons of other churches.

The form of church government is an opinion. There are three basic church polities by which churches are governed: congregational, presbyterial, and episcopal. The words "Deacon," "Elder," "Presbyter" and "Bishop" are all in the New Testament. Wesley was convinced that while each ecclesiastical title can find some scriptural basis, neither can be exclusively correct.

---

240 Wesley, John, Sermon, *"Catholic Spirit,"* JWW Vol. 2, 84.

The way we receive the Lord's Supper and the interpretation we give partaking of the loaf and the cup are opinions. Neither can prove the other to be in grave error. Jesus clearly said, "This is my body...this is my blood," but he also said, "Do this in remembrance of Me."

The modes of baptism are opinions. Scripture can be found, either in word or circumstantial evidence to document baptism by sprinkling, pouring, or immersion. So long as we believe that the efficacy in the sacrament is the presence of the Holy Spirit, the amount of water is not the issue. "Each," Wesley insisted, "acts according to the light that you have."

All agree that baptism is initiation into the faith community of the church, but whether baptism represents totally divine initiative, as in infant baptism, or the faith of the one being baptized, as in adult baptism, is a matter of opinion. Both theologies have their favorite proof texts! Wesley was acquainted with the Quakers who fear that a sacrament can become like an idol; so they do not baptize or celebrate the Lord's Supper. He plans to meet Quakers in heaven!

In his sermon, "The Means of Grace," Wesley did not mention the doctrine of predestined election and universal grace. This divided him and George Whitefield for years, but if you read his eulogy at Whitefield's memorial service, you will know that they finally agreed that this doctrine was not important enough to break their bond of love.

Wesley had a political opinion; he was a Tory. Therefore, he supported the king and opposed the American Revolution. Wesley wrote a very political tract called *A Calm Address to the American Colonies* that was anything but calm! Perhaps one reason he "walked that back" was because Wesley knew that before he was born, his parents separated because of politics. He did not want to hang the future of Methodism on partisan politics. Therefore, on September 10, 1784, he sent a letter to the local preachers in America in which he rose above his politics:

"By a very uncommon train of providence, many of the

provinces of North America are totally disjointed from
their Mother country and erected into independent States.
In this peculiar situation, some thousands of the inhabi-
tants of these states desire my advice..." He then stated he
had broken with his Anglican tradition and ordained two
lay preachers 'sending them as laborers in the vineyard.'
He endorsed the "new reality" in this way: "They (the
former colonies) are now at full liberty, simply to follow the
Scriptures and the Primitive Church. And we judge it best
that they should stand fast in that Liberty wherewith God
has so strangely made them free... If anyone will point out
a more rational and scriptural way of deeding and guiding
these poor sheep in the wilderness, I will gladly embrace it.
At present I cannot see any better method than that I have
taken." [241]

This was a monumental compromise for Wesley and a
significant one to avoid letting his politics become an encum-
brance to his ministry. Monsieur Maurice de Talleyrand of
France, a contemporary of Wesley's, said famously, "A wise
man must adopt the principle of compromise and must not
accommodate the compromise of principle."

No barrier can be too high for Christians to reach over
and embrace – "the principle of compromise." This is the
same supreme ethic that Wesley called "the catholic spirit."
Benjamin Franklin is famous for saying, "We must all hang
together, or most assuredly, we shall all be hanged separately."
Unity in opinions must never replace the principles of truth.

In almost every century, there is a very emotionally divi-
sive social justice issue – slavery, suffrage, divorce, temperance, racial segregation, abortion, immigration, pacificism,
environmental stewardship, climate change, marijuana legal-
ization, sanctuary cities, denial of constitutional rights based
on race, gender, sexual orientation, marital status, etc., etc.,
etc. History shows that the social justice issues that divide one

---

241 Bucke, Emory Stevens, Ed., *The History of American Methodism*, Vol. I, Abingdon,
1964. 203 .

generation seem resolved in the "court of public opinion" by the next.

What about the salvation of good people who are of religious faiths that are not Christian? Look at Wesley's track record. He became "pastor" to the Portuguese Jews in Savannah because they had no Rabbi. He found common ground with the Native Americans. He insisted that all people are children of God, even those whom he called the "Mahomets."

From 1972-2020, The United Methodist Church has seen our sisters and brothers in The Episcopal Church, The Presbyterian Church U.S.A., The Evangelical Lutheran Church of America, the United Churches of Christ, and other Christian denominations divided over one or several of the dimensions of homosexuality. Can United Methodism find a way forward to "stay in love?" Will the "catholic spirit" prevail or will we break fellowship?

J. B. Phillips gave a perennially apropos title to an important little volume for English and American Christians during the years when the Nazis ruled Germany: *Is Your God Too Small?* If we love the Lord with all our heart, mind, soul, and strength and our neighbor as ourself, we best follow the wise advice of Dr. Leslie Weatherhead, a Methodist pastor in London during World War II – "Place that issue on a shelf in our mind and label it, 'waiting further light' and see if we can love our way through our differences of conviction. This is the conscience of Wesley's "catholic spirit."

This has been a list that is partially eighteenth century and partially twenty-first century but the principle is the same. It was over these kinds of divisions that he reasoned, "We might not think alike, but we can love alike." However, he flat out contradicted a prevailing "loosey-goosey" religious attitude of his day – latitudinarianism! Those of that persuasion might be described in words we understand as being "a mile wide and an inch deep." (Technically, the term in Wesley's day meant "total freedom of opinion, conduct, or action.")

It is grossly off the mark to describe John Wesley as one

who had the convictions of a chameleon. He cautioned,

"You do not know of what spirit you are if you call your-selves men of a catholic spirit only because you are of a muddy understanding; because your mind is all in a mist; because you have no settled, consistent principles, but are for jumbling all your opinions together... Go first and learn the first elements of the gospel of Christ; and then shall you learn to be of a truly catholic spirit." [242]

Wesley's Definition of 'Catholic Spirit'

Wesley listed what he considered to be the characteristics of the "catholic spirit." Here is what he calls us to: [243]

1. **"First, please love me."** He insisted that this is more personal than to say, "Love humanity." "No," he said, "love me with tender affection; love me as a friend who is closer than a brother." (Pardon his chauvinistic language!)

2. **"Love me with a love that is not provoked by my follies or infirmities, or even my acting not according to the will of God."** He quotes some of the attributes of love that Paul itemizes in I Corinthians 13.

3. **"Thirdly, commend me to God in all your prayers;** pray that God will speedily correct what he sees amiss and supply what is wanting in me. Pray that the love of God might be more largely poured into my heart."

4. **"Provoke me to love and to good works.** Help me amend my faults, strengthen my weaknesses, build me up in love and make me more fit for the Master's use."

5. **"Love me not only in word, but in deed and in truth."** [244]

In his preface to *Collection of Hymns for the People Called Methodists,* Wesley used a rather picturesque and delightful

---

242 Op. Cit., Wesley's Sermon, *"Catholic Spirit,"* JWW, Vol 2, 93.

243 Ibid., 90.

244 Ibid., Wesley's Sermon, *"Catholic Spirit,"* JWW, Vol. 2, 90-92.

term to describe his doctrine: "a little body of experimental and practical divinity." [245]

Dr. Robert Cushman agreed with that phraseology so much that he entitled his book about Methodist doctrine, *John Wesley's Experimental Divinity*. Son of a bishop and professor at Duke Divinity School for many years, Dr. Cushman said of the phrase, "experimental divinity":

"Never has the leadership of an emerging branch of Protestant Christianity more truly relied upon its hymnal in ecclesial expression to teach doctrine and so to inculcate its salient doctrinal norms. The Wesleys, in an unprecedented measure supplied their followers with the means to sing the Creed. What survives today of the 'experimental and practical divinity' is the continuing usage of that hymnody. It is now our business to identify the differences between the catholic spirit of doctrinal understanding on the one hand and the ever-recurrent 'orthodoxy' or 'true opinion' on the other. Orthodoxy, as we have seen, Wesley viewed as all but superfluous." [246]

---

245 Op. Cit., Cushman, 88.

246 Ibid., Cushman, 88-89 (slightly rephrased in some of Dr. Cushman's longer sentences).

Wesleyan Grace Theology
Epilogue

This little volume is intended to be indicative, not limitingly definitive, and certainly not exhaustive. The best format would be to leave blank pages for you to write your own additional chapter of what is "fundamental" for you.

Too little has been said here about social justice. That is a dimension of perfecting grace that needs its own treatment in another volume. Once when I equated Wesley's term "social holiness" with "social justice," Dr. Richard Heitzenrater corrected me! He insisted that to Wesley, Christianity cannot be a solitary religion of "love of neighbor" but must proactively express itself as acts of mercy and deeds of kindness. However, except for his support of William Wilberforce in the latter's effort to abolish slavery in Great Britain through an act of Parliament, Wesley did not protest most legal norms in his day. What Wesley did do, though, was to infuse within his legacy a proactive spirit of societal reform.

Including a chapter on baptism is not justifiable by the standards of Methodist history. Wesley did not include baptism in his lists of "means of grace." However, the growth of churches who practice only "believer's baptism" makes this sacrament a source of exploration and conflict in many United Methodist families. Baptism has been articulated and emphasized since 1972 when the denomination's first official "Study Commission" spent a quadrennium at work!

Adding a chapter on "catholic spirit" is in response to the "fightings and fears within and without" of The United Method-

227

ist Church as we approach the report of a "Way Forward Study Commission" and the 2020 General Conference. We seem to have a very difficult time with Wesley's question, "Though we may not think alike, can we not love alike?"

My fondest hope is to hear that Sunday School classes, small groups of diverse names and settings, individual laity, and clergy will find these pages helpful. As a pastor for sixty-three years and a saddened heart with the current "winds of divisions," I can see this book as a contemporary primer for looking again at "who we are." Every Christian needs to "... continue to work out your salvation with fear and trembling, for it is God who works in you to will and to act in order to fulfill his good purpose." (Philippians 2:12-13 {NIV})

May the Holy Spirit use this as a helpful tool in leading you to "a faith that will not shrink," but will inform your choices and, through God's grace, sustain you "in the gaps" as the seasons of life unfold. Let this be a springboard to deeper and better sources.

Bibliography

A. Primary Works

Richey, Russell; Rowe, Kenneth; Schmidt, Jean; *The Methodist Experience in America: A Sourcebook, Vols. I & II,* Abingdon 2010

Outler, Albert C. Ed., John Wesley, *A Library of Protestant Thought Series.* New York:Oxford University Press, 1964. Abbreviation: John Wesley

Richey, Russell; Rowe, Kenneth; Schmidt, Jean; *The Methodist Experience in America – A History, Vol. I,* Abingdon, 2010

Richey, Russell; Rowe, Kenneth; Schmidt, Jean, *The Methodist Experience in America – A Sourcebook, Vol. II,* Abingdon, 2000

The Holy Bible quotations are from the *New International Version* unless otherwise cited in the text.

Young, Carlton, Ed., *The United Methodist Hymnal,* 1989

Olson, Harriett, Ed., *United Methodist Book of Discipline,* The United Methodist Publishing House, 2012

B. Select Editions and Compends of John Wesley's Works

The Bicentennial Edition of the Works of John Wesley. 35 volumes projected. Editor in chief, Frank Baker. Publisher: Abingdon Press. Abbreviation in footnotes: JWW

Vol. 1:	Sermons 1.	Ed. Albert C. Outler, 1984
Vol. 2:	Sermons 2.	Ed. Albert C. Outler, 1985
Vol. 3:	Sermons 2	Ed. Albert C. Outler 1986
Vol. 4:	Sermons 4	Ed. Albert C. Outler 1987

Vol. 11: *The Appeals to Men of Reason and Religion and Certain Related Open Letters.* Ed. Gerald R. Cragg, 1975

Vol. 13 *Doctrinal and Controversial Treatises II,* , Eds. Chilcote, Paul; Collins, Kenneth, Abingdon, 2013

Vol. 18: *Journals and Diaries I,* 1735-38. Eds. W. Reginald Ward & Richard P. Heitzenrater, 1988

Vol. 19: *Journals and Diaries II,* 1738-43. Eds. W. Reginald Ward & Richard P. Heitzenrater, 1990

Vol. 22 *Journals and Diaries V,* 1765-75. Eds. W. Reginald Ward & Richard P. Heitzenrater, 1993

Vol. 24 *Journals and Diaries VII,* 1787-179.1 Eds, W. Reginald Ward & Richard P. Heitzenrater, 2003

C. Systematic Works

Miley, John, *Systematic Theology,* Hunt & Eaton, 1893; Hendrickson Publishers, 1989, Vols. I & II

D. Letters and Articles

Benoit, J.D., *Calvin et let baptieme des infants, Revue d'historie et de Philosophie religieuses,* 1937.

Collins, Kenneth, *Wesley's Life and Ministry,* The Cambridge Companion of John Wesley, Cambridge Press

O'Day, Gail, *The Gospel of John – Introduction, Commentary, and Reflections, The New Interpreter's Bible,* Vol. IX, Abingdon, 1995.

Vickers, Jason, *Wesley's Theological Emphases,* The Cambridge Companion of John Wesley, Cambridge Press, 2010

E. Books

Abraham, William, *Waking from Doctrinal Amnesia,* Abingdon, 1995

à Kempis, Thomas, *Imitation of Christ,* Revell, 1953

Barth, Karl, *The Knowledge of God and the Service of God,* Hodder and Stoughton, 1933, 21

Benoit, J.D., "Calvin et le baptemê dos entants." In the *Revue d'Historie et de Philosophie religion ses,* 1937.

Bucke, Emory Stevens, *The History of American Methodism,* Abingdon Press, Vols. I, II, III, 1964

Campbell, Ted A., *Methodist Doctrine – The Essentials,* Abingdon, 1999

Carder, Kenneth L., *Living Our Beliefs – The United Methodist Way,* Abingdon, 1993

Clephane, Elizabeth, (1830-186) Edinburgh, Scotland (printed in local daily paper)

Colaw, Emerson, *Beliefs of a United Methodist Christian,* Tidings, 1972

Cullman, Oscar, *Baptism in the New Testament,* SCM Press, 1961

Cushman, Robert E., *John Wesley's Experimental Divinity,* Kingswood, 1989

Davies, Rupert, *Methodism,* Epworth Press, 1985

Donne, John, *Sermon # 75 preached to Earl of Carlisle,* 1622

Harmon Nolan B., *Understanding the Methodist Church,* Abingdon, 1961

Harper, Steve, *John Wesley's Message for Today,* Zondervan, 1983

Hatch, Nathan; Wigger, John; Eds., *Methodism and the Shaping of American Culture,* Kingswood, 2001

Heitzenrater, Richard, *The People Called Methodists,* Abingdon, 1995

Jones, E. Stanley, Internet, source not given (quotation by Dr. E. Stanley Jones on p. 146)

Jones, Scott, *United Methodist Doctrine – The Extreme Center,* Abingdon, 2002

Langford, Thomas A. *Practical Divinity,* Abingdon, 1983

Lewis, Edwin, *A Christian Manifesto,* Abingdon, 1934

Lewis, Edwin, *The Faith We Declare,* Cokesbury, 1939

Luccock, Halford; Hutchinson, Paul; Goodloe, Robert, *The Story of Methodism,* Abingdon, 1926

MacCullough, Diarmaid, *Christianity – the First Three Thousand Years,* Viking, 2010

Maddox, Randy, *Responsible Grace,* Abingdon, Kingswood, 1994

Maddox, Randy *Rethinking Wesley's Theology*

Maddox, Randy; Vickers, Jason, Eds., *The Cambridge Companion to John Wesley,* Cambridge, 2010

Manning, B. J., *Why Not Abandon the Church?,* London:Independent Press, 1949

Mitchell, Robert, *Castaway Kid,* Tyndale House, 2007

*Muelder, Walter, *Ethics and the Interior Life, New Christian Advocate,* June 1957, 18-22

Oden, Thomas C. , *John Wesley's Teachings, Vol 2,* Zondervan, 2012

Olson, Roger, *Arminian Theology-myths and realities,* IVP Academic, 2006

Outler, Albert, *Evangelism and Theology in the Wesleyan Spirit,* Dischipleship Resources, 2000

Outer, Albert, *John Wesley,* Oxford Press, 1964

Outler, Albert, *Theology in the Wesleyan Spirit, Discipleship Resources,* 1975

Paul, Robert, *The Atonement and the Sacraments,* Abingdon, 1960

Payton, James, *Light from the Christian East,* IVP, 2007

Phillips, J. B., *Letters to the Young Churches,* Macmillan, 1956

Rowe, Gilbert, *The Meaning of Methodism,* Cokesbury Press, 1926

Schweitzer, Albert, *Out of My Life and Thought,* Johns Hopkins University Press, 1933

Smith, H. Shelton, *Faith and Nurture,* Scribners,1941

Stanglin, Keith and McCall, Thomas, *Jacob Arminius,* Oxford, 2012

Sweet, Leonard, *11,* David C. Cook, 2008

Telford, John, *The Letters of the Rev. John Wesley,* Epworth Press, 1931, Vols I-VIII

Thompson, Francis, Morehouse Publishing (no date)

Thorsen, Don, *Calvin vs. Wesley,* Abingdon, 2013

Walker, Williston, *A History of the Christian Church,* 1985,

Walls, Jerry; Dongell, Joseph, *Why I am Not a Calvinist,* IVP, 2004

Warren, Rick, *The Purpose Driven Life,* Zondervan, 2002

Warren, Rick, *The Purpose of Christmas,* Howard Books, 2008

Wesley, John, *Explanatory Notes Upon the New Testament*

Weems, Lovett, *John Wesley's Message Today,* Abingdon, 1992

Williams, Colin, *John Wesley's Theology Today,* Abingdon, 1989

Wynkoop, Mildred Bangs, *Wesleyan Arminianism,* Beacon Hill, Kansas City, 1967

Young, William, *The Shack,* Windblown Media, 2007

Yrigoyen, Charles, *Belief Matters,* Abingdon, 2001

Other books from
Market Square Books

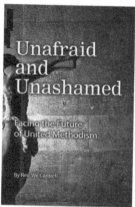

**A Christian Teenager's Guide
To Surviving High School**
Ashley Connor

Unafraid and Unashamed
Facing the Future of United Methodism
Wil Cantrell

IMPACT!
Reclaiming the Call of Lay Ministry
Kay Kotan and Blake Bradford

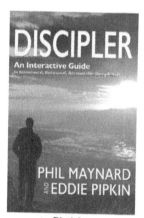

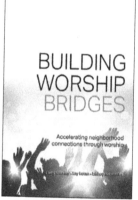

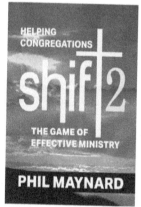

Discipler
An Interactive Guide
Phil Maynard and Eddie Pipkin

Building Worship Bridges
Cathy Townley, Kay Kotan,
and Bishop Robert Farr

Helping Congregations Shift 2
the Game of Effective Ministry
Phil Maynard

—— marketsquarebooks.com ——